UTTOXETER TO BUXTON

via Ashbourne

Vic Mitchell & Keith Smith

MP Middleton Press

Front cover: Class 5 4-6-0 no. 45305 passes Buxton Signal Box with a Tyseley-Buxton special on 23rd October 2010. (J.Whitehouse)

Back cover (upper): Class 7F 0-8-0 no. 49262 waits at Parsley Hay on 14th June 1962. The porter appears to have loaded coal into his barrow for a station fire. (D.L.Dott/Colour-Rail.com)

Back cover (lower): Railway Clearing House map, dated 1947.

Published September 2019
First reprint February 2021

ISBN 978 1 910356 33 3

Cover design Deborah Esher
Typesetting & Design Cassandra Morgan

Published by
> *Middleton Press*
> *Easebourne Lane*
> *Midhurst*
> *West Sussex*
> *GU29 9AZ*
Tel: 01730 813169
Email: info@middletonpress.co.uk
www.middletonpress.co.uk

Printed and bound by CPI Group (UK) Ltd, Croydon, CR0 4YY

INDEX

ACKNOWLEDGEMENTS

We are very grateful for the assistance received from many of those mentioned in the credits, also from A.J.Castledine, G.Croughton, G.Gartside, A.C.Hartless, J.Hinson (Signalling Record Society), J.Horne, C.M.Howard, J.Langford, N.Langridge, B.Lewis, D. and Dr S. Salter, T.Walsh, the Mayfield Heritage Group and, in particular, our always supportive families.

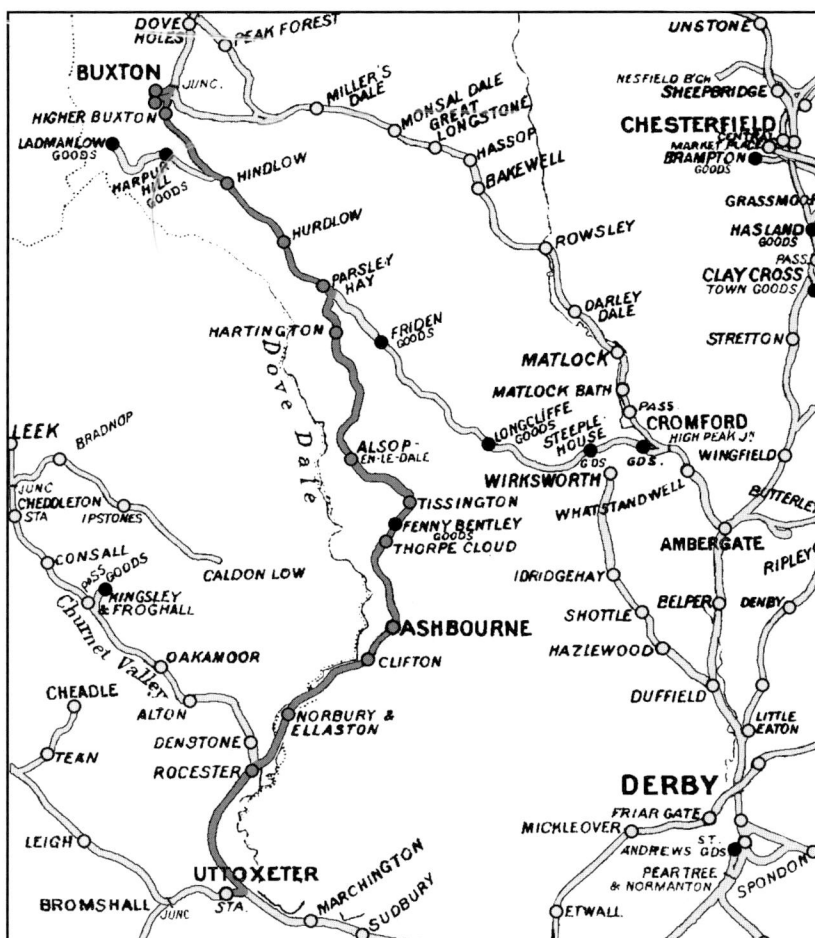

1. The bold line shows our route on this
Railway Clearing House map from 1947.

GEOGRAPHICAL SETTING

Flowing west, south of Ashbourne, is Henmore Brook and north of it is Benter Brook. Both soon run into the River Dove. This flows south at the foot of the Pennine Hills, while our line runs roughly close to it, whilst climbing steeply onto the hills, for about 12 miles.

Initially, the route was built on sandstones and mudstones, but after a few miles it climbed onto the limestones of the Pennines. This once housed a substantial number of small lead mines. The Peak District National Park was established to cover most of this area, which is entirely in Derbyshire. The first two stations herein were just in Staffordshire.

The maps are scaled at 25ins to 1 mile, with north at the top, unless otherwise indicated.

HISTORICAL BACKGROUND

The lines north, east and west of Uttoxeter were opened in 1848-49 by the North Staffordshire Railway. It operated from Rocester to Ashbourne from 31st May 1852. The line from Parsley Hay to Buxton was opened on 1st June 1894: between Hindlow and Parsley Hay it was built on the 1830 Cromford & High Peak Railway, which was amalgamated with the London & North Western Railway on 19th July 1887. Opened on 4th August 1899, the LNWR line from Ashbourne to Parsley Hay was intended to be part of an alternative route from London to Manchester. Both the LNWR

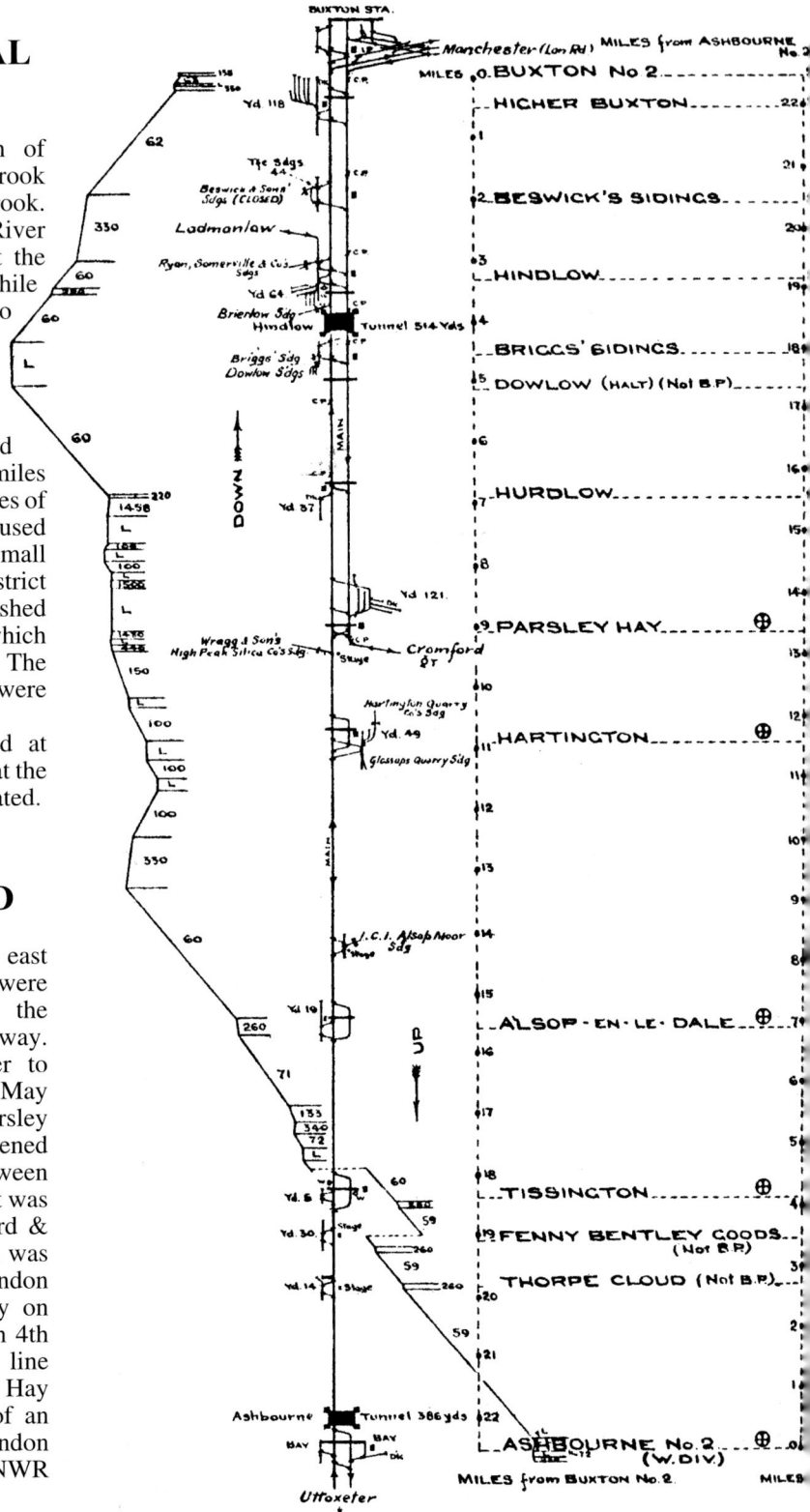

BUXTON STA.

Manchester (Lon Rd)   MILES from ASHBOURNE

MILES   0 BUXTON No 2

HIGHER BUXTON   22

BESWICK'S SIDINGS

HINDLOW

Tunnel 514 Yds

BRIGGS' SIDINGS

DOWLOW (HALT) (Not B.P.)

HURDLOW

PARSLEY HAY

Cromford Gt

HARTINGTON

J.C.I. Alsop Moor Sdgs

ALSOP-EN-LE-DALE

TISSINGTON

FENNY BENTLEY GOODS (Not B.R.)

THORPE CLOUD (Not B.R.)

Ashbourne   Tunnel 386 yds

ASHBOURNE No. 2 (W. DIV.)

MILES from BUXTON No.2

Uttoxeter

and the Midland Railway had reached Buxton, from the north and east respectively, in June 1863. Both companies became part of the London Midland & Scottish Railway at the Grouping in 1923. This formed most of the London Midland Region of British Railways upon Nationalisation in 1948.

Passenger services between Rocester and Buxton were withdrawn on 1st November 1954, though, until 7th October 1963, the LMR ran an annual Sunday excursion from Manchester to Ashbourne to coincide with the well-dressing ceremonies at Tissington and other villages in the neighbourhood. Winter emergency services ceased from this date also.

Connected lines and freight withdrawals are given in the captions. Private sidings all closed on 2nd October 1967.

The trackbed from Ashbourne to Parsley Hay was acquired by Derbyshire County Council and the Peak District National Park in 1968 for a cycle and walking route.

PASSENGER SERVICES

The 1865 timetable for services between Rocester Junction and Ashbourne showed four weekday trains and two on Sundays. By 1883 the figures were six and two, and in 1899 they were nine and three.

The Parsley Hay-Buxton service of November 1894 offered just two trains, weekdays only. More came after the route was completed, in 1899. The 1901 service is shown herein in two timetables, as in *Bradshaw*. There were later some slip coaches on offer, giving a direct service from Euston to Buxton on this route. Two weekday slips were shown in 1910; they ran until 1914.

July 1899

DERBY, BURTON, UTTOXETER, LEEK, ASHBOURNE, MACCLESFIELD, STOKE, and CREWE.—North Staffordshire.

	Week Days.																					Sundays.					
	mrn	mrn	mrn	mrn	mrn	mrn	Thro' to Chester and North Wales.	mrn	mrn	mrn	mrn	aft	aft	mrn	aft	aft	aft	aft	aft	aft	aft	mrn	mrn	mrn		aft	aft
St. Pancras, London 418....dep.	....	....	....	....	5 15	....		....	....	....	1035	....	Wednesdays and Saturdays.	1035	....	1225	2 0	4 0	4 0	....	Saturdays only.	....	....	1130		3 15	....
Leicester 418. "	....	....	....	....	7 27	....		10 0	....	10 0	1245	....		1245	....	2 50	4 4	6 13	6 13	....		....	....	1 47		5 33	....
441 Nottingham.... "	....	....	6 25	....	7 47	....		1015	....	1015	1 20	....		1 25	....	3 5	4 10	6 12	6 12	....		....	....	1 55		5 15	....
Derby.............dep.	....	6b36	7 40	....	9 0	....		1110	....	1130	2 5	....		2 35	....	4 25	5 20	7 5	7 5	....		....	9 0	4 15		6 30	....
262 London (K.C.)..dep.	....	....	....	....	5 15	....		....	....	....	10 0	....		....	....	1035	1230	3 25	3 25	....		....	....	1130		1130	....
272 Nottingham.... "	....	5 48	....	....	7 57	....		9 53	9 53	....	1238	....		....	....	2 50	3 43	6 10	6 10	....		....	7 50	2 55		3g45	....
Egginton Junction	....	6 51	7 58	....	9 16	....		1127	1132	1146	....	....		....	....	4 41	5 39	7 21	7 21	....		....	9 20	4 34		6 47	....
310 London (Euston) dep	....	....	....	....	5 15	....	7 10	Thro' to Chester and North Wales	....	....	8 45	....		....	....	12 0	1 30	4 0	4 0	....		....	....	....		....	....
Burton (Station St.) dp	....	....	7 40	....	9 0	....	11 0		....	....	2 0			2 40	....	4 25	5 25	7 0	7 0		9 0	....	9 0	....		6 30	8 10
Horninglow	....	....	7 44	....	9 4	....	11 4		....	....	2 4			2 44	....	4 29	5 29	7 4	7 4		9 4	....	9 4	....		6 34	8 14
Rolleston-on-Dove ..	....	....	7 49	....	9 9	....	11 9		....	....	2 9			....	....	4 34	5 34	7 9	7 9		9 9	....	9 9	....		6 39	8 19
Tutbury ....arr.	....	....	7 55	....	9 15	....	1115		....	....	2 15			2 53	....	4 40	5 40	7 15	7 15		9 15	....	9 15	....		6 45	8 25
Tutbury	....	6 57	8 11	....	9 24	....	1117		1138	1153	2 27	Thursdays and Saturdays.		3 0	....	4 49	5 48	7 29	7 29	Thursdays and Saturdays.	Stop	....	9 30	4 44		6 57	Stop
Sudbury	....	7 4	8 21	....		....	1124		1144	12 0	2 35			3 7	....	4 57	5 57	7 37	7 37			....	9 40	4 54		7 8	
Marchington	....	a	8 26	....		....	1129		1149	12 6	....			....	....	5 2	6 2	....	....		....	....	9 45	4 59		7 13	....
Uttoxeter 272....arr.	—	7 11	8 32	....	9 36	....	1134	1144	....	1212	2 44			....	....	5 8	6 7	7 45	7 45		....	....	9 51	5 5		7 19	....
Uttoxeter.......dep.	8 10	7 16	9 20	....	10 0	....	....		....	1230	3l0		3 0	3k15	....	5 30	6 14	8 0	8j10		....	....	1010	5 15	6 40	7 30	....
Rocester	8 22	7 24	9 28	....	10 8	....	....		....	1238	3l8		3 8	3k23	....	5 39	6 23	8 8	8j18		aft	....	1018	5 24	6 48	7 38	....
Rocester......dep.	8 30	....	....	....	1010	1130	....		....	1243	3l10		....	3k25	4 50	5 43	6 24	....	8j20		9 0	....	1025	5 26	....	7 39	....
Norbury	8 37	....	....	....	1018	d	....		....	1250	3l18		....	3k33	4 57	5 50	6 31	....	8j27		9 7	....	1032	5 35	....	7 46	....
Clifton (Mayfield)..	8 45	....	....	....	1026	d	....		....	1258	3l26		....	3k41	5 5	5 58	6 39	....	8j35		9 14	....	1040	5 44	....	7 54	....
Ashbourne....arr.	8 49	....	....	....	1030	1145	....		....	1 2	3l30		....	3k45	5 9	6 2	6 42	....	8j39		9 18	....	1045	5 48	....	7 58	....
Churnet Valley. Denstone Crossing...	Stop	c	9 33		....	Stop	....		....	1244	....		3 13	3 30	Stop	5 45	Through Carriage to Ashbourne.		....			....	....	Stop	6 54	....	
Alton		7 33	9 39		....	....	....		....	1250	....		3 19	3 36		5 52		8 17	....			....	....		7 1	....	
Oakamoor	....	7 39	9 44		....	....	....		....	1256	....		3 24	3 41	....	5 58			....			....	....	....	7 7	....	
Froghall	....	7 46	9 51		....	....	....		....	1 3	....		3 31	3 47	....	6 5			....			6 0	....	....	7 14	....	
Cheddleton	....	7 56	10 0	Tuesdays and Fridays.	....	....	....		....	1 13	....	aft	3 40	3 56	....	6 14			....			6 10	....	....	7 23	....	
Leek 405........	....	8 3	10 6		....	....	....		....	1 22	....	3 4	3 48	4 3	....	6 21		Saturdays only.	....	9 14	Saturdays only.	6 17	....	....	7 32	....	
Rudyard	....	8 11	1011		....	....	....		....	1 28	....	3 9	3 54	4 9	....	6 27			....	9 19		6 23	....	....	7 39	....	
Rushton	....	8 19	1018		....	....	....		....	1 35	....	3 16	4 1	4 16	....	6 35			....	9 26		6 30	....	....	7 47	....	
Bosley	....	8 25	1024		....	....	....		....	1 41	....	Stop	4 7	4 21	....	6 41			....			6 36	....	....	7 53	....	Change at Stoke.
North Rode Junc. 408	....	8 33	1030		....	....	....		....	1 47	....		4 15	4 27	....	6 47			....	....		6 48	....	....	8 0	....	
Macclesfield (Cen.)..	....	8 43	1039		....	....	....		....	1 56	....	....	4 25	4 37	....	6 57			....	....		6 58	....	....	8 10	....	
" (Hibel Road)	....	8 44	1040		....	....	....		....	1 57	....	....	4 27	4 39	....	7 0			....	....		7 0	....	....	8 12	....	
Buxton * 402 ..arr.	h	1017	1254		....	....	....		....	3 35	....	....	7 20	....	....	8 30	....		....	....		9h28	....	....	....	....	
403 M'chestr L.& N.W.	....	9 35	1135		....	....	....		....	2 40	....	....	6 40	6 40	....	8 15	....		....	....		8 23	....	....	9 0	....	
529 London Rd Gt. Cen.	....	9 52	1137		....	....	....		....	3 40	....	aft	6 52		....	8 5	....		....	....		9 33	....	....	1023	....	
Uttoxeter..........dep.	....	7 30	8 37		9 40	....	1150		....	1225	2 48	2 55	....	Saturdays only.	aft	5 13	....	....	7 49	Sats. only	....	....	9 55	....	....	7 26	
Leigh	For other Trains, p. 408.	7 42	8 49		....	....	....		....	1236		3 9	....		3e40	5 27	aft	....	....		aft	....	10 7	....	....	7 42	
Cresswell	....	7 49	8 56		....	....	....		....	1244	....	3 16	....		3c50	5 35	6 42	....	....		1030	....	1014	....	....	7 52	
Blyth Bridge	....	7 55	9 1		....	....	....		....	1249	....	3 21	....		3 55	5 40	6 47	....	....		1035	....	1019	....	....	7 59	
Meir	mrn	7 58	....		....	mrn	....		....		....	3 26	....		3 58	....	6 52	....	....		1040	....	....	aft	....	....	aft
Normacot	7 0	8 1	....	9 25	....	1130	....		....	....	....	3 30	....		4 0	....	6 56	....	....		1045	....	1025	2 0	....	8 6	10 5
Longton.........	7 3	8 4	9 10	9 30	10 5	1133	1215		....	1257	3 14	3 33	....		4 3	5 49	7 0	....	8 15		1048	....	1029	2 3	....	8 11	10 8
Fenton	7 7	8 8	....	9 35	....	1136	....		....	....	....	3 36	....		4 6	....	7 3	....	....		1051	....	1032	2 6	....	8 15	1011
Stoke 408.... arr.	7 10	8v11	9v16	9v39	1010	1141	1220		....	1v2	3 20	3 39	....		4v11	5 56	7v9	....	8 20	v	1056	....	1040	2v15	....	8v24	1018
404, 409 dep.	7 15	8o25	9 25	9 45	1015	1145	1224		....	1e45	3 25	3 41	....		4 30	6 1	7 23	....	8 25	....	11 5	....	1045	3 5	....	8 28	11 5
Etruria (Basford)...	7 19	8 30	9 28	9 50	....	1150	....		....	1e49	....	3 44	....		4 34	6 6	7 26	....	....	....	11 8	....	1050	3 9	....	8 33	....
Longport †	7 24	8 35	9 33	9 55	1022	1154	....		....	1e54	3 31	....	....		4 39	6 12	7 30	....	8 32	....	1113	....	1055	3 14	....	8 39	....
Chatterley	7 29	8 40	9 37	....	....	1158	....		....	1e59	....	....	....		4 44	6 17		....	....	....	....	....	11 0	3 19	....	8 45	....
Harecastle ‡ 409....	7 34	8 45	9 42	10 2	1029	12 2	1236		....	2e4	3 37	....	....		4 49	6 23	7 36	....	8 39	....	1119	....	11 5	3i30	....	8 52	1118
Alsager (Rode Heath).	7 40	8 52	*Via* Macclesfield.	....	1035	12 7	....		....	....	3 43	....	....		4 55	6 29	7 41	....	8 45	....	1124	....	1111	3 36	....	9f5	1124
Radway Green	7 44	8 57		....	....	1211	....		....	....	....	....	....		5 0	6 34	....	....	....	....	....	....	1116	3 40	....	*Via* Macclesfield.	....
Crewe 311, 401....arr.	7 52	9 7		1015	1045	1220	1250		....	....	3 53	....	....		5 9	6 45	7 50	....	8 55	....	1135	....	1125	3 49	....		1135
Chester 358...arr.	9 5	9 47		....	1155	....	1 36		....	....	4 32	....	....	....	6 0	8 30	8 30	....	9 40	....	1234	....	3 40	9 50	....		1234
387 Liverpool (L.S.) "	9 35	1025		1115	12 5	....	2 0		....	....	5 45	....	....	....	6 30	8 20	9 20	....	1010	....	1240	....	4 5	6 10	....		3 10
401 Manchester (L.R.) "	9 26	11 2	1047	1115	1215	1 42	2 0		....	....	5 27	....	....	....	6 10	8 5	9 10	....	1012	....	1 25	....	3 55	9 57	....	1036	1 5

NOTES.

- **a** Stops to set down from G.N. Stations, and to take up for West of Uttoxeter.
- **b** Departs from G.N. Station.
- **c** Stops on Wednesdays to take up.
- **d** Stops to set down on informing the Guard at Rocester.
- **e** Saturdays only.
- **f** To Alsager Road Station, changing at Harecastle.
- **g** Change at Kimberley.
- **h** *Via* Stockport, L. & N. W.
- **i** Change at Harecastle.
- **j** Runs 20 minutes later on Saturdays.
- **k** Wednesdays and Saturdays.
- **l** Runs 15 minutes later on Wednesdays and Saturdays.
- **o** Through to Chester and North Wales.
- **v** Change Trains.
- * *Via* Middlewood.
- † Station for Wolstanton.
- ‡ Station for Kidsgrove.

DERBY, BURTON, UTTOXETER, LEEK, ASHBOURNE, MACCLESFIELD, STOKE, and CREWE.—North Staffordshire.

Down. | **Week Days.** | **Sundays.**

Timetables for January 1901.

Tables from October 1912 can be found underneath pictures 79 and 80.

NOTES.

a Stops to set down from G. N. Stations, and to take up for West of Uttoxeter.

b Departs from G. N. Station.

c Stops on Wednesdays to take up.

d Stops to set down on informing the Guard at Rocester.

e Saturdays only.

h Via Stockport, L. & N. W.

f Change Trains.

k Stop to set down from London (Euston) on informing the Guard at Burton.

l Runs 15 minutes later on Wednesdays and Saturdays.

* Via Middlewood.

† Station for Wolstanton.

‡ Station for Kidsgrove.

§ Victoria Station.

Right-side notes:

a Stops to set down from Crewe and beyond.

d Stops to take up for Harecastle, Longport, or Stoke.

b To Alsager Road, changing at Harecastle.

c Change at Harecastle, via Stockport, L. & N. W.

e Change Trains.

Station list (Down):

St. Pancras, London 458 ..... dep.
489 Nottingham ......
Derby ..... dep.
294 London (K.C.) ......
304 Nottingham § ......
Egginton Junction ......
344 London (Euston) dep.
Burton (Station St.) dep.
Horninglow ......
Rolleston-on-Dove ......
Tutbury ..... arr.
Tutbury ......
Sudbury ......
Marchington ......
Uttoxeter 304 ..... arr.
Uttoxeter ..... dep.
Rocester ......
Rocester ..... dep.
Norbury ......
Clifton (Mayfield) ......
Ashbourne 439 arr.
Buxton 439 arr.
Denstone Crossing ......
Alton ......
Oakamoor ......
Froghall ......
Cheddleton ......
Leek 444 ......
Rudyard ......
Rushton ......
Bosley ......
North Rode June. 447 ......
Macclesfield (Cen.) ......
„ (Hibel Road) ......
Buxton * 438 arr.
437 M'chestre / L. & N. W.
577 Londn Rd | Gt. Cen.
Uttoxeter ..... dep.
Leigh ......
Cresswell ......
Blyth Bridge ......
Meir ......
Normacot ......
Longton ......
Fenton ......
Stoke 447 arr. / dep.
442, 443
Etruria (Basford) ......
Longport ......
Chatterley ......
Harecastle ‡ 448 ......
Alsager (Rode Heath) ......
Radway Green ......
Crewe 345, 435 ..... arr.
Chester 392 ..... arr.
423 Liverpool (L. & I.) ......
435 Manchester (L. R.) ......

ASHBOURNE, BUXTON, WHALEY BRIDGE, NEW MILLS, and MANCHESTER.—L. & N. W.

Fares. | **Return.** | **Down.**

1 cl. | 2 cl. | gov | 1 cl. | 2 cl. | gov

Station list (Down):

Ashbourne ..... dep.
Thorpe Cloud, for Dovedale ......
Tissington ......
Alsop-en-le-Dale ......
Hartington ......
Parsley Hay ......
Hurdlow ......
Hindlow ......
Higher Buxton ......
Buxton 476 to 481 { arr. / dep.
Dove Holes ......
Chapel-en-le-Frith ......
Whaley Bridge ......
Furness Vale ......
New Mills 576 ......
Disley [577 ......
Middlewood, for High Lane ......
Bollington ......
Macclesfield * 577, 447 ar.
Hazel Grove ......
Davenport [427, 437, 417 ......
Stockport 352, 428, 434 ar.
437 Macclesfield † ..... arr.
Crewe 436 ......
Chester 392 ......
427 Liverpool (Lime St.) „
Heaton Norris ......
Heaton Chapel ......
Levenshulme and Burnage ......
Longsight (Belle Vue) ......
Manchester 418, 412 arr.

Continued below.

Down—Continued.

Ashbourne ..... dep.
Thorpe Cloud, for Dovedale ......
Tissington ......
Alsop-en-le-Dale ......
Hartington ......
Parsley Hay ......
Hurdlow ......
Hindlow ......
Higher Buxton ......
Buxton 476 to 481 { arr. / dep.
Dove Holes ......
Chapel-en-le-Frith ......
Whaley Bridge ......
Furness Vale ......
New Mills 576 ......
Disley [577 ......
Middlewood, for High Lane ......
Bollington ......
Macclesfield * 577, 447 ar.
Hazel Grove ......
Davenport [427, 437, 417 ......
Stockport 352, 428, 434 ar.
437 Macclesfield † ..... arr.
Crewe 435 ......
Chester 392 ......
427 Liverpool (Lime St.) „
Heaton Norris ......
Heaton Chapel ......
Levenshulme and Burnage ......
Longsight (Belle Vue) ......
Manchester 418, 412 arr.

* Central Station. **†** Hibel Road Station. For **Local Trains** between Stockport and Manchester, see page 44.

a Stops to set down Season Ticket Holders. **b** Saturdays only. **c** Arrives at 5 22 aft. on Saturdays. **e** Wednesdays, Thursdays, and Saturdays. **g** Arrives at 3 20 aft. on Saturdays. **h** Except Saturdays. **i** Arrives at Bollington at 2 34 and Macclesfield at 2 29 aft. on Saturdays.

ASHBOURNE and UTTOXETER.—L. M. & S.

Miles	Up.	Week Days. mrn	mrn		mrn	mrn	mrn		aft		aft		aft	aft		aft	Sundays. aft			
	420 Buxton ....dep.	....	7 25	....	9s20	....	10 42	....	....	....	1k45	....	....	5 53	....	8 10	3 45	....	....	....
—	**Ashbourne**............dep.	7 34	9 5	....	10s45	....	11 42	....	1 50	....	4 20	....	5s35	7 13	....	9 20	6 0	....	....	....
1½	Clifton for Mayfield	7 37	9 8	....	10s48	....	11 45	....	1 53	....	4 23	....	5s38	7 16	....	9 28	6 4	....	....	....
4½	Norbury and Ellaston	7 44	9 15	....	10s54	—	11 51	....	2 0	....	4 31	....	5s44	7 18	....	9 30	6 11	....	....	....
6¾	Rocester 521..............	7 50	9 21	....	11s0	11 21	11 57	....	2 6	....	4 37	....	5s50	7 28	....	9 36	6 17	....	....	....
11¼	**Uttoxeter 523, 532**..arr.	8 8	9 31	....	....	11 31	12 7	....	2 15	....	4 47	....	6s0	7 37	....	9 46	6 28	....	....	....
24¼	522 Burton-on-Trent A arr.	9 27	1036	....	....	1a18	1 18	....	3 17	....	6 3	....	....	8 40	....	10s57	8 0	....	....	....

Miles	Down.	Week Days. mrn	mrn	mrn	mrn	mrn		aft	aft	aft		aft	aft	aft				Sundays. aft			
	Station Street, 523 Burton-on-Trent ..dep.	7 10	9 9	....	....	10v43	....	1 40	2s30	2e30	....	5s25	....	7 5	....	....	....	5 50	....	....	....
—	**Uttoxeter**............dep.	8 15	1025	10e33	....	12 55	....	3 0	5s0	5e43	....	6s20	6 45	8 30	....	....	....	7 35	....	....	....
4½	**Rocester**..................	8 29	1033	10e41	11s22	1 3	....	3 8	5s8	5e51	....	6s28	6 57	8 38	....	....	....	7 43	....	....	....
7	**Norbury and Ellaston**	8 35	1041	10e49	11s28	1 11	....	3 16	5s16	6e0	....	6s36	7 3	8 46	....	....	....	7 52	....	....	....
10	**Clifton for Mayfield**	8 42	1049	10e57	11s35	1 19	....	3 24	5s24	6e8	....	6s44	7 11	8 54	....	....	....	7 58	....	....	....
11½	**Ashbourne 421**........arr.	8 47	1054	11e2	11s40	1 24	....	3 29	5s29	6e13	....	6s49	7 14	9 59	....	....	....	8 3	....	....	....
33¾	421 Buxton ....arr.	1020	1233	....	....	2 45	....	5 19	....	....	....	....	9 2	....	....	....	....	....	....	....	....

A Station Street. *a* Arrives at 12 18 aft. on Saturdays. *e* Except Saturdays. *k* Departs at 2 30 aft. on Saturdays.
s Saturdays only. *v* Departs at 11 50 mrn. on Saturdays.

September 1925

ASHBOURNE, HARTINGTON, and BUXTON.—L. M. & S.

Miles	Down.	Week Days. mrn	mrn	mrn	mrn	aft	aft	aft	aft S		Sundays. aft			
—	**Ashbourne**............dep.	7 45	9 15	1112	....	1 30	4 10	7 45	....	....	6 10	....	....	....
2¾	Thorpe Cloud **F**	7 52	9 22	1119	....	1 37	4 17	7 52	....	....	6 18	....	....	....
4	Tissington..................	7 58	9 29	1125	....	1 43	4 23	7 58	....	....	6 25	....	....	....
6¾	Alsop-en-le-Dale **F**	8 8	9 39	1138	....	1 51	4 32	8 8	....	....	6 34	....	....	....
11	Hartington..................	8 20	9 48	1150	....	2 3	4 43	8 19	....	....	6 46	....	....	....
13¼	Parsley Hay................	8 26	9 53	1156	....	2 11	4 49	8 26	8 50	....	6 54	....	....	....
15¼	Hurdlow **D**	8 31	10 0	12 8	....	2 21	4 55	8 33	8 55	....	7 2	....	....	....
18¼	Hindlow	8 40	10 8	1217	....	2 30	5 6	8 42	9 3	....	7 11	....	....	....
21¼	Higher Buxton	8 47	1015	1225	....	2 38	5 14	....	....	....	....	....	....	....
22¾	**Buxton 566** ....arr.	8 53	1020	1233	....	2 45	5 19	9 2	9 18	....	7 25	....	....	....

NOTES.

D Station for Longnor (3 miles) and Monyash (1½ miles).
E Except Saturdays.
F Station for Dovedale.
S Saturdays only.

UTTOXETER and ASHBOURNE

Miles	Down HOUR	Wk Days mrn 8	9		12	3	S 5	E 5	7	aft S 8	Sun.	aft 3	6	
—	**Uttoxeter**..........dep.	23	56	.	50	12	10	43	0	36	.	0	35	.
4½	Rocester..................	30	**3**	.	57	19	17	50	8	43	.	8	43	.
7	Norbury and Ellaston....	37	10	.	**4**	26	24	57	16	50	.	15	50	.
10	Clifton, for Mayfield......	44	17	.	11	33	31	**4**	23	57	.	27	57	.
11½	**Ashbourne 523** .....arr.	49	23	.	16	38	36	9	28	**2**	.	34	**2**	.

Miles	Up HOUR	Week Days mrn 7	9	11		1	4		7	aft S 9		Sun	aft 6	
—	**Ashbourne**.........dep.	25	2	36	.	40	25	.	20	15	.	.	0	.
1½	Clifton, for Mayfield....	28	5	39	.	43	28	.	24	18	.	.	3	.
4½	Norbury and Ellaston....	35	12	46	.	50	35	.	31	25	.	.	10	.
6¾	Rocester **519**...........	41	18	52	.	56	41	.	37	31	.	.	16	.
11½	**Uttoxeter 526, 528**.arr.	50	28	**1**	.	**5**	50	.	45	40	.	.	25	.

E Except Sats. S Sats only

March 1938

BUXTON and ASHBOURNE

Miles	Up HOUR	Week Days mrn 7	8	S 9	10	E 1	S 1	S 3	S 6	E 5	S 5	aft S 7	Sundays aft 4			
—	**Buxton**.............dep.	7	.	15	35	45	55	15	.	5 53	5 53	50	4 48	..	..	..
½	Higher Buxton...........	10	.	17	37	47	57	17	.	5 55	5 55	..	..	..	..	..
3½	Hindlow	18	.	26	46	56	**6**	26	.	6 4	6 4	59	..	..	..	..
4½	Dowlow Halt.............	22	.	30	50	**0**	10	30	.	6 8	6 8	**3**	.	..	..	..
6¾	Hurdlow **D**	27	.	35	55	5	15	35	.	6 13	6 13	8	..	..	..	..
9	Parsley Hay..............	33	0	41	**4**	11	21	41	.	6 19	6 19	14	5 13	..	..	..
10¾	Hartington...............	.	5	46	9	16	26	46	.	6 24	6 24	22	5 18	..	..	..
15½	Alsop-en-le-Dale **F**......	.	15	55	18	25	35	54	10	6C34	6C38	31	5F33	..	..	..
18¼	Tissington	.	22	**1**	24	31	41	**1**	16	6N43	6U50	37	5H45	..	..	..
19¾	Thorpe Cloud **F**	.	27	6	29	36	46	6	21	6 48	6 55	42	5 50	..	..	..
22½	**Ashbourne 572**.......arr.	.	32	11	34	41	51	11	26	6 53	7 0	47	5 55	..	..	..

Miles	Down HOUR	Week Days mrn 7	10		S 11		1		4	S 5		7	aft S 9		Sundays aft 7			
—	**Ashbourne**..........dep.	50	28	.	8	.	35	.	18	40	.	50	15	.	7 5	..	..	..
2¾	Thorpe Cloud **F**.........	57	35	.	16	.	43	.	26	48	.	57	23	.	7 13	..	..	..
4	Tissington................	**4**	41	.	26	.	49	.	32	54	.	**4**	29	.	7 19	..	..	..
6¾	Alsop-en-le-Dale **F**......	14	49	.	36	.	57	.	40	**1**	.	12	37	.	7 27	..	..	..
11½	Hartington...............	24	58	.	48	.	**6**	.	49	.	.	21	46	.	7 36	..	..	..
13¼	Parsley Hay..............	28	**2**	.	52	.	10	.	53	.	.	25	50	.	7 40	..	..	..
15½	Hurdlow **D**	33	7	.	59	.	15	.	58	.	.	30	55	.	..	..	..	..
17¾	Dowlow Halt..............	39	13	.	**5**	.	21	.	**4**	.	.	36	**1**	.	..	..	..	..
18¾	Hindlow..................	42	16	.	8	.	24	.	9	.	.	40	5	.	..	..	..	..
21¾	Higher Buxton	50	24	.	16	.	32	.	17	.	.	.	.	.	..	..	..	..
22½	**Buxton** ....arr.	53	28	.	19	.	35	.	20	.	.	47	12	.	8 3	..	..	..

A Newtown; about ¾ mile to Midland Section and L. & N. E. Station. **B** South; over 1 mile to Central Station. **C** Station for Golf Links. Alighting Platform only. C Arr. 6 31 aft **D** For Longnor (3 miles) and Monyash (1½ miles). 0 Arr. 6 43 aft. **E** Except Sats. **F** For Dovedale. F Arr. 5 26 aft. H **Arr. 5 38 aft.**
H Change at Stockport. K South Junc. Platform. **L** Sats. only. One cl. only N Arr. 6 39 aft. P Mayfield. **S** or S Sats. only. **T** Stops to take up.
U Dep 2 18 aft on Sats. Z On 27th inst. only. Z Dep 9 30 aft on Sats., changing at Stockport.

Where the MINUTES under the Hours change to a LOWER figure and DARKER type it indicates the NEXT HOUR.

UTTOXETER and ASHBOURNE

Miles		Week Days only a.m		a.m F		Sats. only p.m		Except Sats. p.m F		Sats. only p.m F		p.m	
—	Uttoxeter.............dep	8 28	..	10 0	..	1 20	..	3 45	..	3 55	..	6 17	..
4½	Rocester..................	8 35	..	10 7	..	1 27	..	3 52	..	4 2	..	6 24	..
6¾	Norbury and Ellaston......	8 42	..	1014	..	1 34	..	3 59	..	4 9	..	6 31	..
10	Clifton, for Mayfield.......	8 49	..	1021	..	1 41	..	4 6	..	4 16	..	6 38	..
11½	Ashbourne............arr	8 54	..	1027	..	1 46	..	4 11	..	4 21	..	6 43	..

Miles		Week Days only a.m		a.m F	a.m F		Sats. only p.m		Except Sats. p.m		Except Sats. p.m F	Sats. only p.m F
—	**Ashbourne**............dep	7 20	..	8 47	1122	..	3 30	..	4 5	..	6 55	7 25
1½	Clifton, for Mayfield......	7 23	..	8 50	1125	..	3 33	..	4 8	..	6 59	7 29
4½	Norbury and Ellaston......	7 30	..	8 57	1132	..	3J45	..	4J20	..	7 6	7 37
7	Rocester...................	7 38	..	9 3	1138	..	3 51	..	4 26	..	7 12	7 43
11½	Uttoxeter.............arr	7 47	..	9 12	1147	..	4 0	..	..	..	7 21	7 52

F Through Carriages to or from Buxton (Table 127)
J Arrives 5 minutes *earlier*

May 1953

MANCHESTER, BUXTON and ASHBOURNE

Mls. from Buxton		Week Days only a.m T		a.m T		p.m ET		p.m ST	
	126 Manchester (L.Rd.) dep	..	..	9 0	..	4 45	..	5 5	..
—	Buxton................ dep	7 7	..	1025	..	5 55	..	6 20	..
3¼	Hindlow	7 16	..	1034	..	6 4	..	6 29	..
4¾	Dowlow Halt..............	7 20	..	1038	..	..	..	..	..
9	Parsley Hay..............	7H59	..	1047	..	6 18	..	6 43	..
10¾	Hartington	8 4	..	1054	..	6 23	..	6 48	..
15½	Alsop-en-le-Dale **B**	8 14	..	11 2	..	6 31	..	6 56	..
18¼	Tissington................	8 20	..	11 8	..	6 40	..	7 5	..
19¾	Thorpe Cloud **B**..........	8 24	..	1112	..	6 44	..	7 9	..
22½	**Ashbourne** ....arr	8 30	..	1118	..	6 50	..	7 15	..

Miles		Week Days only a.m		a.m T		p.m ET		p.m ST	
—	Ashbourne ....dep	7 50	..	1035	..	4 18	..	4 25	..
2¾	Thorpe Cloud **B**	7 57	..	1042	..	4 25	..	4 32	..
4¼	Tissington................	8 5	..	1051	..	4 31	..	4 38	..
7	Alsop-en-le-Dale **B**	8 13	..	11K3	..	4 38	..	4 45	..
11¾	Hartington	8 23	..	1113	..	4 48	..	4 55	..
13½	Parsley Hay...............	8 28	..	1118	..	4 55	..	5 0	..
17¾	Dowlow Halt..............	8 37	..	1127	..	5 4	..	..	..
19¼	Hindlow	8 40	..	1130	..	5 7	..	5 12	..
22¼	Buxton.............. arr	8 50	..	1140	..	5 17	..	5 22	..
47¾	**126 Manchester (L.Rd.) arr**	9 48	..	2U17	..	6 49	..	6 49	..

B For Dovedale
E Except Saturdays
H Arr. 7 28 a.m.
K Arr. 10 58 a.m.
S Saturdays only
T Through Carriages between Buxton and Uttoxeter (Table 131)
U Arr. Mayfield Station 1 48 p.m. on Saturdays

UTTOXETER

Schools
Bradley House
Alleyne's Grammar School
268
N.S.R.
CHURNET BRANCH
S.Ps
BRADLEY STREET
BACK LANE
L.B.
SILVER STREET
Bank Terrace
Smy
Brewery
Tank
CHURCH STREET
Vicarage
Grave Yard
St. Mary's Church
(Vicarage)
B.M.257·3

UTTOXETER

Cross
(Site of)
MARKET PLACE
B.M.264·2
QUEEN STREET
P.H.
MARKET STREET
BRIDGE STREET
Temperance Hall
Cheese Factory
BROOKSIDE
P.H.
P.H.
STATION ROAD
S.Ps
Schs
S.B.
S.P.
Cheese Fact
Leighton Iron Works
Timber Yard
West Junction
B.M.274·9
Tank
Brook Furlong
Goods Station
S.P.
S.P.
W.M.
Pinfold Crossing
S.P.
Sluice
S.B.

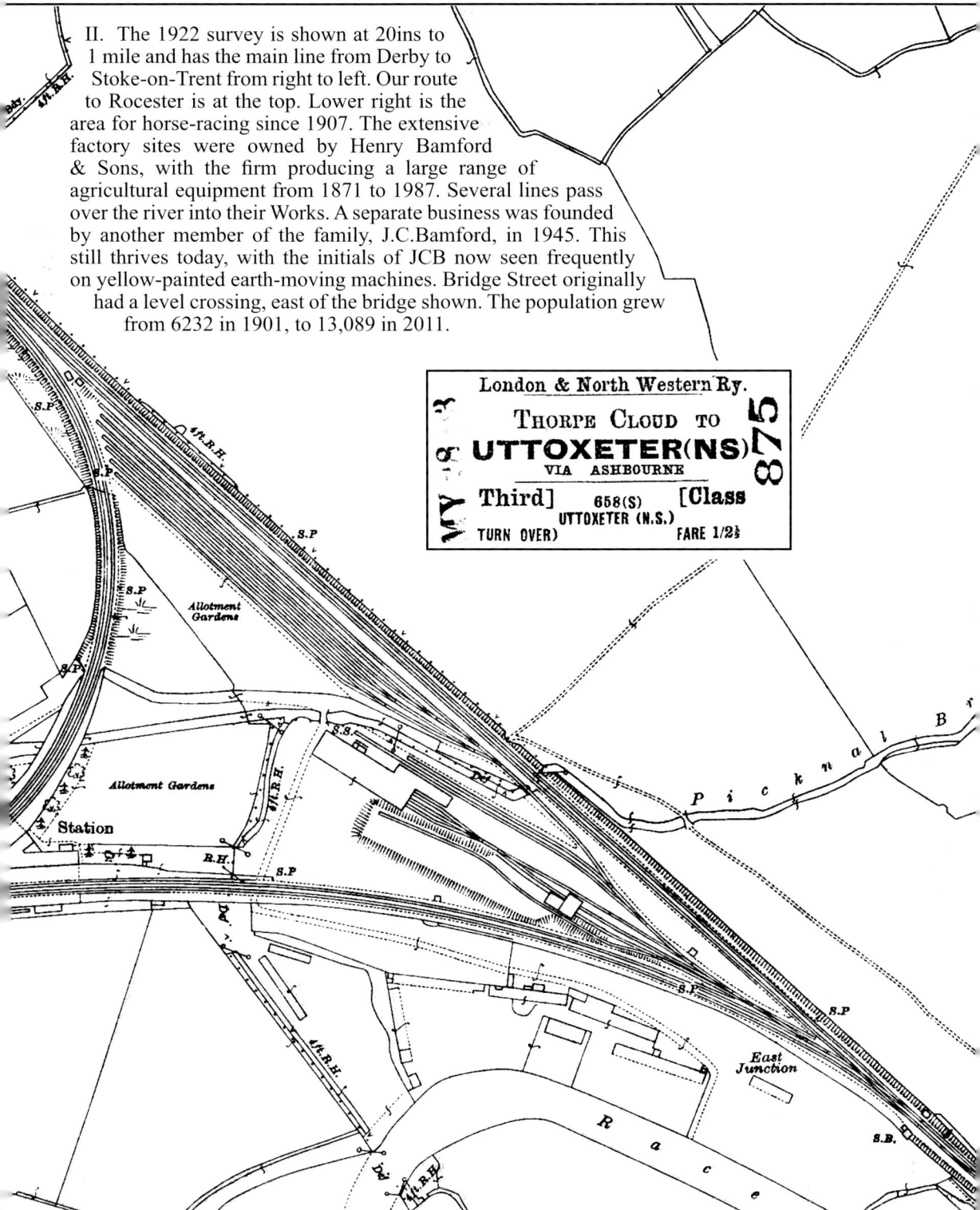

II. The 1922 survey is shown at 20ins to 1 mile and has the main line from Derby to Stoke-on-Trent from right to left. Our route to Rocester is at the top. Lower right is the area for horse-racing since 1907. The extensive factory sites were owned by Henry Bamford & Sons, with the firm producing a large range of agricultural equipment from 1871 to 1987. Several lines pass over the river into their Works. A separate business was founded by another member of the family, J.C.Bamford, in 1945. This still thrives today, with the initials of JCB now seen frequently on yellow-painted earth-moving machines. Bridge Street originally had a level crossing, east of the bridge shown. The population grew from 6232 in 1901, to 13,089 in 2011.

London & North Western Ry.

THORPE CLOUD TO
UTTOXETER(NS)
VIA ASHBOURNE

Third] 658(S) [Class
UTTOXETER (N.S.)
TURN OVER)   FARE 1/2½

MY -3

875

Allotment Gardens

S.P

Allotment Gardens

Station

R.H.

S.P

Picknal B?

East Junction

R a c e

S.B.

1.   The first station was close to Bridge Street and was in use from 7th August 1848 to 1st October 1881. Its replacement is seen in 1899, along with gas lights and one smoke hood. It is at the spot where locomotives are likely to dwell and be a nuisance to bridge users. (J.Suter coll.)

2.   NSR 0-6-0T no. 140 seems in fine condition as it waits to depart, prior to 1923. It has a choice of couplings and a square cornered sand box. (J.Alsop coll.)

3.   This NSR 0-6-0T is no. 139 and is seen leaving for Stoke-on-Trent in 1908, hauling six-wheeled coaches. Note that the bridge had been roofed and glazed by that time. The station approach is also evident, in part. (J.Suter coll.)

4.   A view east from the road bridge includes more of the approach road and part of the sidings serving two large warehouses. On the left is West Junction Box and a dock serving milk traffic and also pharmaceutical supplies from Beeston to Boots Warehouse, which was nearby. (LOSA coll.)

5. It is 20th May 1948 and 2-6-4T no. 42665 waits with the 6.24pm from Macclesfield. The train showing the white rear lamp is bound for Leek. Such lamps had red glass. Two more smoke hoods have arrived, but the bridge glass has gone. Passenger services on the Churnet Valley Line from Uttoxeter towards Leek and Macclesfield ceased operation on 2nd January 1965, and the trains towards Ashbourne and Buxton ended on 1st November 1954. The tracks at both platforms on the left were lifted by 1970. (W.A.Camwell/SLS coll.)

← 6. North Box was north of the triangle and controlled the level crossing over the A518, Derby Road. It is seen in April 1959. The box had 29 levers and was open from October 1875 to 30th January 1966. (R.Humm coll.)

For other views, see Middleton Press albums, *Uttoxeter to Macclesfield* and *Derby to Stoke-on-Trent*.

7.   The ex-NSR engine shed can be found on map II near the centre of the triangle on the right page. It had code no. 5F from 1948 until it closed on 7th September 1964. Six or seven locomotives were usually housed here in that period. Top right is the water tank. (D.K.Jones coll.)

8.   Following the closure of the southern end of the Churnet Valley, the up Churnet line between Uttoxeter East and Uttoxeter North was retained as a siding to serve the Shell Mex and BP Oil Depot that had opened in 1961. Upon closure of Uttoxeter East Box in March 1969, the connection was controlled by a ground frame. The weekly oil train from Stanlow ceased running in 1979 and the connection was finally severed on 15th May 1983. A DMU is running in on 10th April 1984, working the 09.20 Crewe to Lincoln. The road bridge is in the background. The one for passengers had been demolished and they had to use the old barrow crossing, in the background. A new footbridge came into use in 2013 and passengers could then reach the racecourse safely. Following privatisation, Central Trains operated the route from 2nd March 1997. East Midlands Trains was the franchisee from 11th November 2007, with East Midlands Railway taking over on 18th August 2019. (P.D.Shannon)

UTTOXETER
DOVE BANK

9. The station opened on 13th July 1849, just north of Derby Road. Its level crossing was controlled by the signal box in the background. Station closure was on the same day as the one at Bridge Street, 1st October 1881. To the north was Spath Crossing, which was the first on BR to be automated. Its lifting barriers were operating from 5th February 1961. (R.Humm coll.)

NORTH OF UTTOXETER

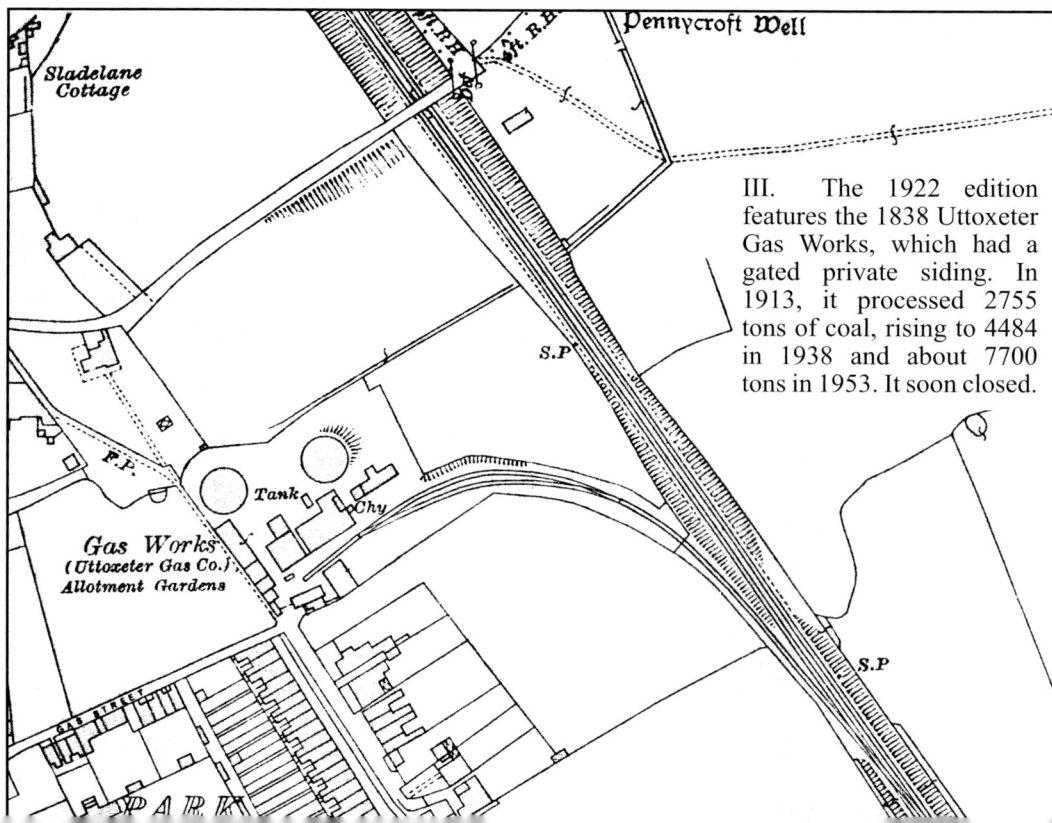

III. The 1922 edition features the 1838 Uttoxeter Gas Works, which had a gated private siding. In 1913, it processed 2755 tons of coal, rising to 4484 in 1938 and about 7700 tons in 1953. It soon closed.

ROCESTER

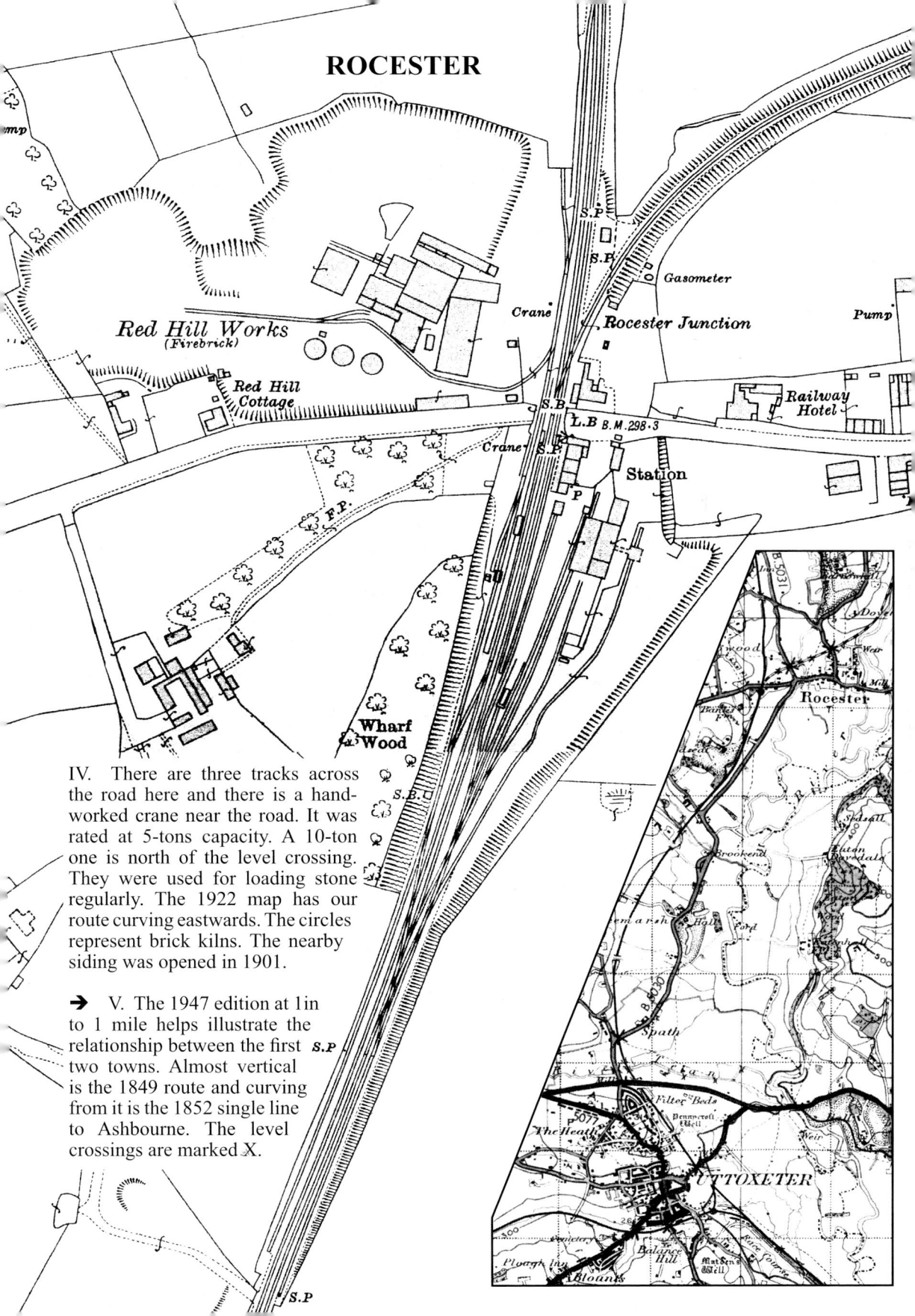

Red Hill Works
(Firebrick)

Red Hill
Cottage

Crane

Rocester Junction

Gasometer

Pump

S.P

S.P

S.B

L.B B.M.298·3

Crane S.B

Station

P

P

Railway
Hotel

F.P.

Wharf
Wood

S.B.

IV. There are three tracks across
the road here and there is a hand-
worked crane near the road. It was
rated at 5-tons capacity. A 10-ton
one is north of the level crossing.
They were used for loading stone
regularly. The 1922 map has our
route curving eastwards. The circles
represent brick kilns. The nearby
siding was opened in 1901.

➜ V. The 1947 edition at 1in
to 1 mile helps illustrate the
relationship between the first
two towns. Almost vertical
is the 1849 route and curving
from it is the 1852 single line
to Ashbourne. The level
crossings are marked X.

S.P

S.P

10.   The signal box had 36 levers and was in use from August 1882 until 21st May 1965. The one shown on the map in Wharf Wood was just a ground frame. On the corner of the ornate building is a sign offering PORTERS. One pair is dealing with two milk churns. (J.Suter coll.)

London & North Western Ry.

TISSINGTON (No.2.) TO

UTTOXETER (NS)

VIA ASHBOURNE

Third 657(NO2)(S) [Class

UTTOXETER(N.S)

TU...(ER) FARE 1/3½

L. & N.W.R.
Available on day of issue only. Not transferable.

RETURN HALF
VOLUNTEER

THIRD CLASS

Ashbourne
TO
TISSINGTON (NO.2)

L. & N.W.R.
Issued subject to the conditions in the Co's Time Tables Books Bills & Notices

OUTWARD HALF
VOLUNTEER

THIRD CLASS

TISSINGTON (No.2)
TO
ASHBOURNE (L&NW)

657 (No2 (VOL)(R)

ASHBOURNE Fare ·4

L. & N. W. R.
Only valid to return from 6.0 a.m. on Sunday (if trains permit) up to Monday night inclusive Not transferable

SATURDAY to MONDAY
THIRD CLASS

Derby (G.N.)
TO
TISSINGTON (No2.)
Via Egginton and Ashbourne

TURNOVER

L. & N.W.R.
Issued subject to the conditions & regulations in the Co's Time Tables & Notices & Excursion and other Bills

SATURDAY to MONDAY
THIRD CLASS
TISSINGTON (No2)
TO
DERBY (G.N.)
Via Ashbourne and Egginton

657 No2 SM

DERBY (G.N.)

L. M. & S. R.
No1 FOR CONDITIONS SEE NOTICES

TISSINGTON TO
ALSOP-EN-LE-DALE

THIRD
CLASS 657 No1(S) FARE -/6 G
ALSOP-EN-LE-D.

11. The gates are open for a train from Ashbourne on this undated postcard. The station had opened on 1st August 1849, when the Churnet Valley line to Leek and beyond opened. 1286 were housed here in 1901 and 1345 in 1961. (J.Alsop coll.)

12. It is 25th April 1948 and class 4 2-6-4T no. 42235 runs in, heading the 5.0pm Uttoxeter to Macclesfield service. To the right of it is the ground frame box and on the left is an early electric light. (SLS coll.)

13. Goods traffic ceased here on 1st June 1964. The smaller goods crane is included herein and centre are the disused gates over the third track. The River Churnet is only ¼ mile distant, which might explain the ground saturation, after rain. (J.Suter coll.)

14. A house was built for the station master, behind the signal box, in 1883. From the back windows he could enjoy trains arriving from Ashbourne, as we do here in about 1954. Blowing off is no. 42667, a class 4 2-6-4T. The larger goods crane is on the left. (R.Humm coll.)

15. Only the platform on the right was used after 1959. This fine panorama is from 17th June 1958. A massive JCB factory now lies across the route, in the background. The station closed on 2nd January 1965, when trains ceased to run to Leek. The van was in use by a contractor. (G.Hunt/Colour-Rail.com)

For other views, see pictures 8 to 11 in *Uttoxeter to Macclesfield*. **They include the prospective passenger's perspective, which is a pleasure to perceive.**

London & North Western Ry. Issued subject to the conditions & regulations in the Cos Time Tables Books Bills & Notices ASHBOURNE TO **ALSOP-EN-LE-DALE** Second] 659(S) [Class ALSOP-EN-LE-D. FARE -/8	**L. M. & S. R.** FOR CONDITIONS SEE NOTICES ASHBOURNE TO **ALSOP-EN-LE-DALE** THIRD CLASS] 659(S) FARE 1/1 C ALSOP-EN-LE-D.

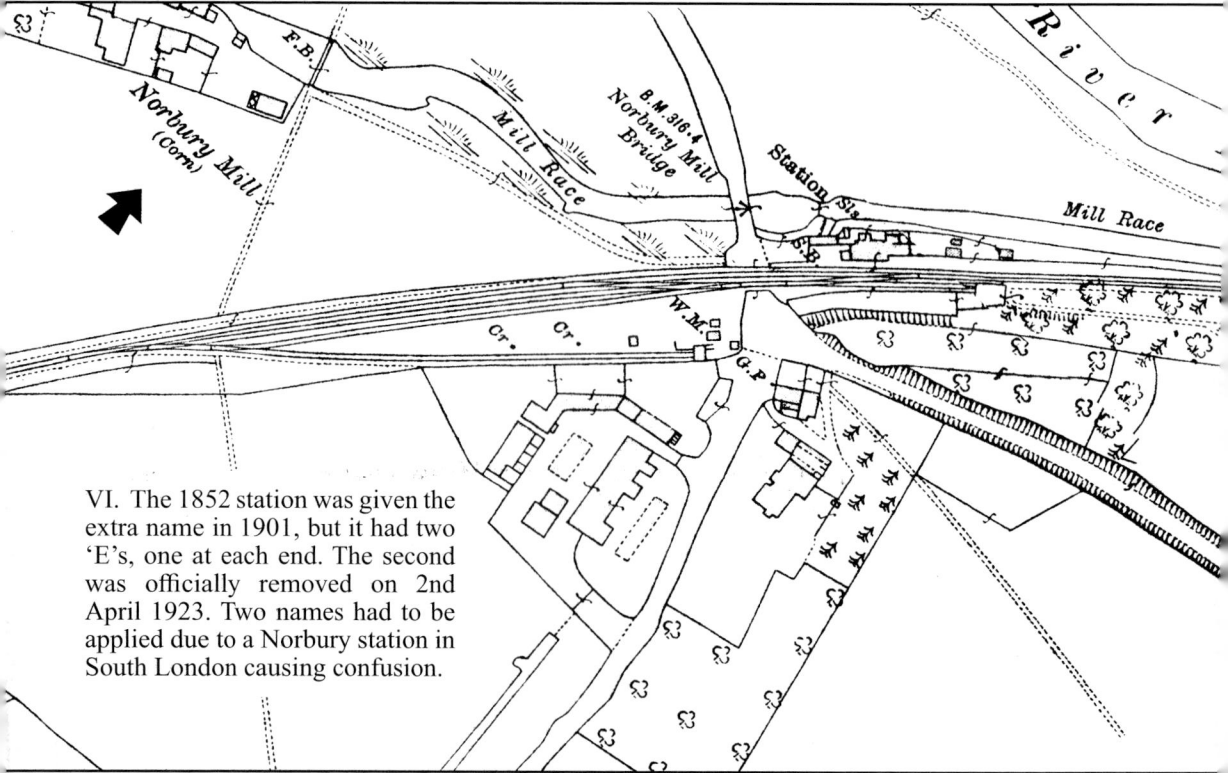

VI. The 1852 station was given the extra name in 1901, but it had two 'E's, one at each end. The second was officially removed on 2nd April 1923. Two names had to be applied due to a Norbury station in South London causing confusion.

16. This postcard was created in 1901-06, with the usual posing of staff and family. Raised platforms were common at that time. The 'Telegrams' signs on the station building showed that you could send and/or receive them here. At many places you could pay for them to be delivered by a station porter. (J.Alsop coll.)

17.   It is 24th April 1954 and nearest is the parcel and luggage store. The fireman is holding out the single line token hoop for the signalman to catch, while 2½ passengers take an interest. (R.J.Buckley/Initial Photographics)

18.   Class 4 2-6-4T no. 42590 calls with an Alsop to Uttoxeter train on 14th September 1954. The signal box had a 20-lever frame and was closed on 1st June 1964. The gates were manually operated. (J.Suter coll.)

19.   Ex-LNWR 0-8-0 no. 49132 runs through on 17th June 1958. Passenger service was withdrawn on 1st November 1954, but goods continued until 1st June 1964. This was thus a rare treat for the photographer. The 1961 census showed 280 souls in Norbury. (H.Davies/Photos from the Fifties)

20. The first bridge here over the River Dove was of timber construction. Its steel replacement is seen under construction in about 1901. What appears to be a third smaller span is just scaffolding. The bridge type is known as 'Tied Arch'. The arch is in compression, whilst the beam is in tension. (J.Alsop coll.)

| 9349 | L. M. & S. R. FOR CONDITIONS SEE NOTICES THORPE CLOUD TO ALSOP-EN-LE-DALE THIRD CLASS] 658(S) FARE -/8 C ALSOP-EN-LE-D. | 9349 |

| 29 SE 29 | London & North Western Ry. Issued subject to the conditions & regulations in the Cos Time Tables Books Bills & Notices. THORPE CLOUD TO ASHBOURNE (L.& N.W.) Third] 658(S) [Class ASHBOURNE FARE -/3 | 2783 |

CLIFTON (MAYFIELD)

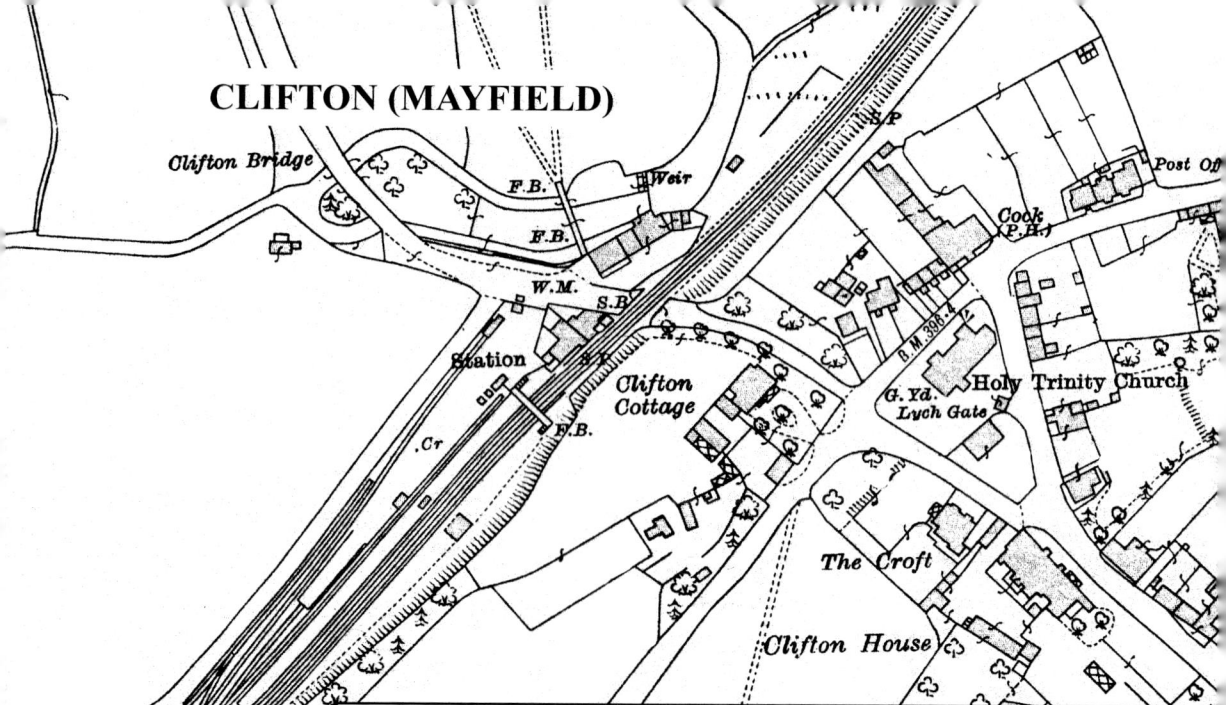

VII. Originally named Clifton, it was renamed Clifton (Mayfield) on 22nd August 1893, but was shown as Clifton for Mayfield in some timetables. The signal box, lower left, was named Clifton Yard. This map is from 1922 and it records a footbridge present. This does not appear in any photograph; it was not on the 1900 map as there was only a single track.

21. This early view was recorded as 1879. Apart from one board bearing CLIFTON, there were no helpful signs for passengers. We are looking northwards. The curve to the left border of the above map was termed Mayfield Siding and the 1938 list refers to W. Tatton & Co. Ltd. (J. Suter coll.)

22.   The panorama is seen southward, but the level crossing is unclear; one post shows and this is clearer in picture 25. Above is a sign bearing TELEGRAMS. The sign in front of the nearby window states: TO BOOKING OFFICE ⇦. The card was post-marked 1904. (P.Laming coll.)

23.   The platform waiting facilities were not provided with heating, but the main buildings had numerous chimneys. Fire buckets are hanging below the window on the right. (R.Humm coll.)

24. Two views from 24th April 1954 from a passenger's camera add to the visit. The 1900 map had shown only three short sidings; one north of the station and two to the south. A van stands on the right one. The map shows that the space on the left of it had carried a track serving an end-loading dock. The 'T' structure carried two loading gauges. (R.J.Buckley/Initial Photographics)

25. The window board states CLIFTON ST^N and this is the last year for seeing it from a train. The gateway to the goods yard is on the right and beyond is the weighbridge office, marked W.M. on map VII. The box had 16 levers and was worked as a ground frame. (R.J.Buckley/Initial Photographics)

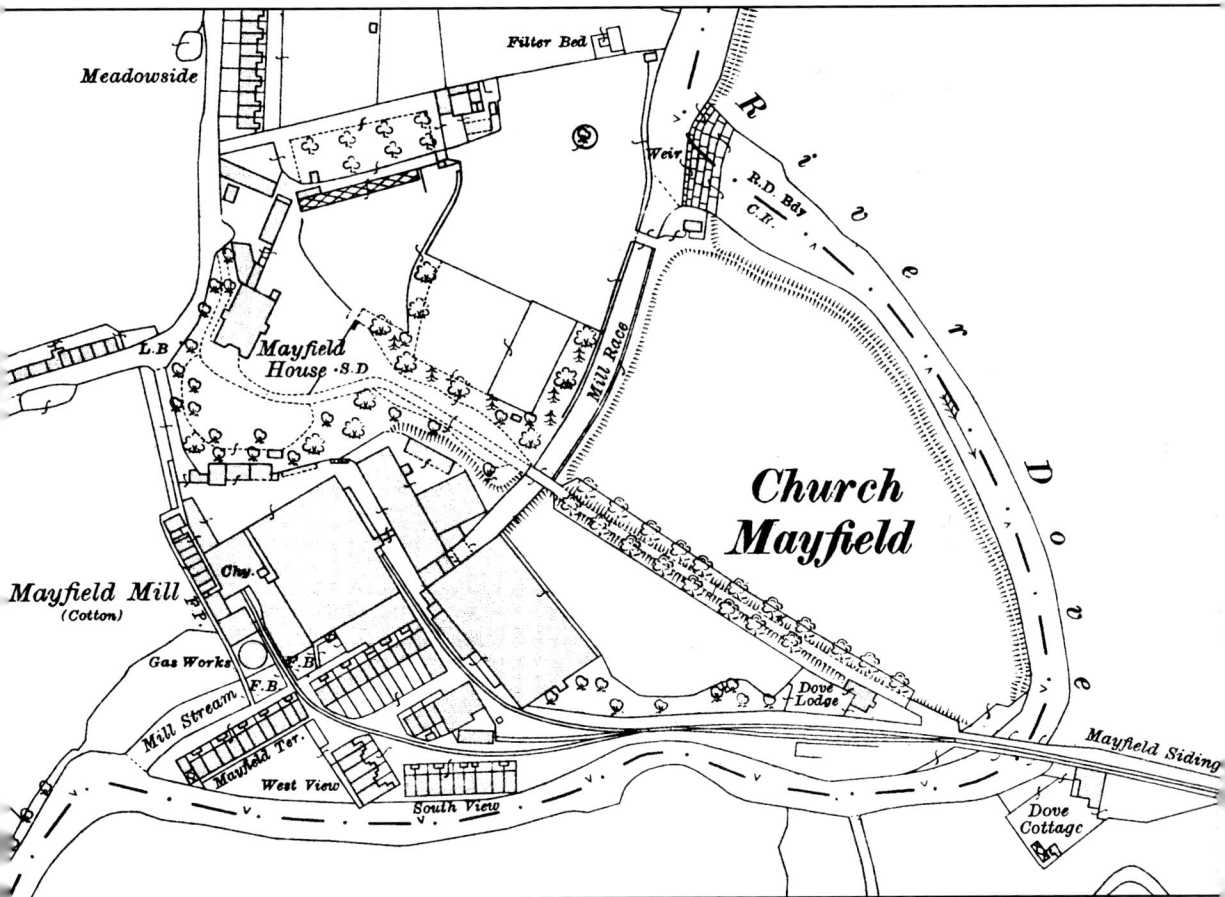

VIII. This is a continuation from the left of the last map. The Mayfield Mill site has the rare distinction of a history of almost 200 years of textile production. The first mention of any sort of mill occurs in a property valuation of 1291: most of Mayfield then belonged to the Priory of Tutbury and it included a corn mill. By 1793 there had been various owners of the site which developed to include two corn mills, two fulling mills and a leather mill. Textiles first appeared in 1795 when the cotton mill was completed. Unfortunately in 1806 the interior of the building, together with most of the machinery, was destroyed in a fire. The spinning of cotton continued until 1934 when it was sold to William Tatton & Company, who used the mill to process silk. Mayfield Yarns were operating from the site in 2019. The Mayfield Heritage Group (*mayfieldheritage.org.uk*) provided many of the details here, along with the photo, right.

Shown above is the siding bridge running into the boiler yard in August 2019. (Mayfield Heritage Group)

26.   Clifton Yard signal box was photographed on 22nd April 1959. It had 27 levers and was usable until 1st June 1964. The foot boards and light were to aid the signalman during token exchanges. The lower window served the machine room. (H.F.Wheeller/R.S.Carpenter coll.)

27.   The goods yard is seen on the same day. It had closed on 4th June 1956, but freight trains continued to pass by to serve Ashbourne until 1964. This panorama was probably seen from the steps of the box in the above picture. (H.F.Wheeller/R.S.Carpenter coll.)

ASHBOURNE

The Laurels

Hill Crest

Old Grammar School

L.B.

B M 407

Almshouses

S.D.

Almshouses

The Mansion

School

Grave Yard

Daisybank

School

B M 404·0

F.B.

Well

St. Oswald's Church
(Vicarage)

Old Almshouses

F.B.

F.P.

F.P.

Grave Yard

Schoolhouse Bridge

66 S 320

S.B.

B.M.400·0

Overflow

S.Ps

Police Station

Oil Tank

F.B.

L.B

Clifton Road

Railway Hotel (P.H.)

Cr. S.P.

Goods Shed

B M 393·6

Oil Tank

Nursery

S.B.

Engine Shed

Tk

S.P

Filter Bed

F.P.

Highfield

F.Bs

S.P

Chy

P

Condensed Milk Factory

L.B

Road

Cheese Factory

Filter

IX. The 1922 edition is shown
at 20ins to 1 mile and has the
station top right. The entrance
to the 378yd long tunnel was
just beyond Church Street,
near the upper border. Single
line prevailed between stations
from here to Parsley Hay. The
small engine shed was an early
creation by the NSR. It was in
use from 1878 to November
1932 and was demolished in
1937. To the left of it is the NSR
signal box, which had 38 levers.
The LNWR box is top right and
is in pictures 30, 31, 37 and 40.

↑ 28. This is the first station and was in use as a terminus until 1899. It was situated in Clifton Road, near the end of the straight tracks and was soon demolished. Road conditions are poor on the left. (R.Humm coll.)

↗ 29. The fresh station is evident, along with a spacious bridge needed to span the new lines to it. Under the structure is a contractor's engine. In this and the next picture, the land for sidings remains empty. They came later. (J.Suter coll.)

→ 30. Opening on 4th August 1899, the station was initially provided with one bay platform, as seen. The small arches on the left are over a drainage channel. The rings on the signal arms indicate that they are for use in shunting procedures only. (R.Humm coll.)

31. The new station had become the joint property of the NSR and the LNWR. Now we can see the fourth platform. The timetables at the front of this album show that many local trains terminated here, for years. (J.Alsop coll.)

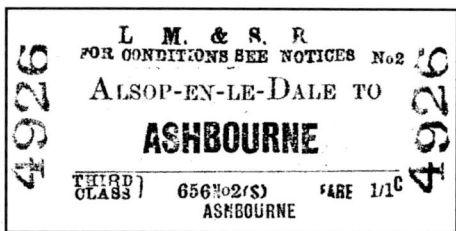

4926
L M. & S. R
FOR CONDITIONS SEE NOTICES No2
ALSOP-EN-LE-DALE TO
ASHBOURNE
THIRD CLASS) 656No2(S)   FARE 1/1C
ASHBOURNE
4926

4862
L.M.& S. For conditions see notices.
MONTHLY RET
Valid as advertised
THIRD CLASS
Buxton
TO No1
ALSOP-EN-LE-DALE
Fare 3/5 C
656No0(MR)
BUXTON
L M. & S. R.
MONTHLYRET
THIRD CLASS
ALSOP-EN-LE-DALE
No1   TO
BUXTON
Fare 3/5 C
4862

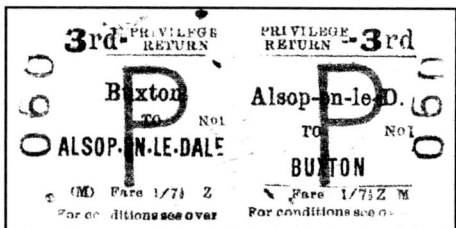

060
3rd PRIVILEGE RETURN
Buxton
TO No1
ALSOP-EN-LE-DALE
(M) Fare 1/7½ Z
For conditions see over
PRIVILEGE RETURN **3rd**
Alsop-en-le-D.
TO No1
BUXTON
Fare 1/7½ Z M
For conditions see o.
060

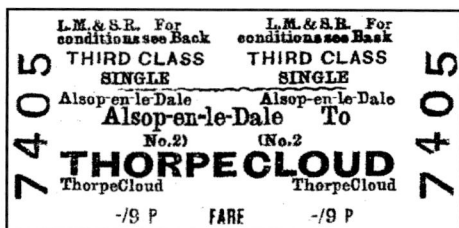

7405
L.M.& S.R. For conditions see Back
THIRD CLASS
SINGLE
Alsop-en-le-Dale
Alsop-en-le-Dale
No.2)
ThorpeCloud
L.M.& S.R. For conditions see Back
THIRD CLASS
SINGLE
Alsop-en-le-Dale
To
(No.2
ThorpeCloud
THORPE CLOUD
-/9 P   FARE   -/9 P
7405

32. In this panorama we look south and it emphasises the severity of the curve leading to the tunnel, which passes under the road. Steaming trains stand in both bay platforms. (P.Laming coll.)

33. This is the scene in about 1914 as local men leave for war. The town's population was 4039 in 1901, rising to 5660 in 1961. Such views were recorded on numerous stations. (P.Laming coll.)

34.   A unique form of pleasure had developed over generations, called the ASHBOURNE GAME. The ball is just carried by the two teams playing the game, known as Up'Ards and Down'Ards (local dialect for 'upwards' and 'downwards'). The Up'Ards are traditionally town members born north of Henmore Brook, which runs through the town, and Down'Ards are those born south of the river. It is only played on two days per annum, Shrove Tuesday and Ash Wednesday. The goals are three miles apart and are formed of mill stones. (P.Laming coll.)

35.   A local train calls on 3rd May 1934, probably from Buxton. No. 2264 was an 0-6-2T, ex-NSR, which was sold to Manchester Collieries and named *Kenneth* in 1936. It was not scrapped until 1964. (H.C.Casserley)

36.   This is no. 122, a 2-6-2T class 3P. It is working the 3.35pm departure to Uttoxeter on 22nd May 1948. It will soon receive BR numbering and lettering. The footbridge has lost its roof. (W.A.Camwell/SLS)

37.   We now have two views from early 1954, after a light snow fall. Snow was so heavy once in 1901 that a train was stuck in it further north, for three days. Local farmers kindly provided hot food and drinks for all its passengers. (R.Humm coll.)

↑ 38. The single track northwards begins in the background and passes under the houses. Both bay buffer stops are visible and on the right is the spacious Station Hotel, which had some fine railway views. It was first called The Beresford Arms and later reverted to this. (R.Humm coll.)

↗ 39. Moving southwards, the hotel is still visible. On the left is the large office block built for the two companies to undertake diverse duties including goods in, goods out, wages and work duties. (W.A.Camwell/SLS)

→ 40. A DMU displaying its 'Cats Whiskers' was selected for one end of the SLS Railtour on 15th April 1961. The trip began and ended at Burton-on-Trent. It gave members time to travel over the C&HPR line, steam-hauled in open wagons, but they had to walk the inclines. The 36-lever ex-LNWR box lasted from about 1901 until line closure.
(D.Lawrence/Photos from the Fifties)

THORPE CLOUD

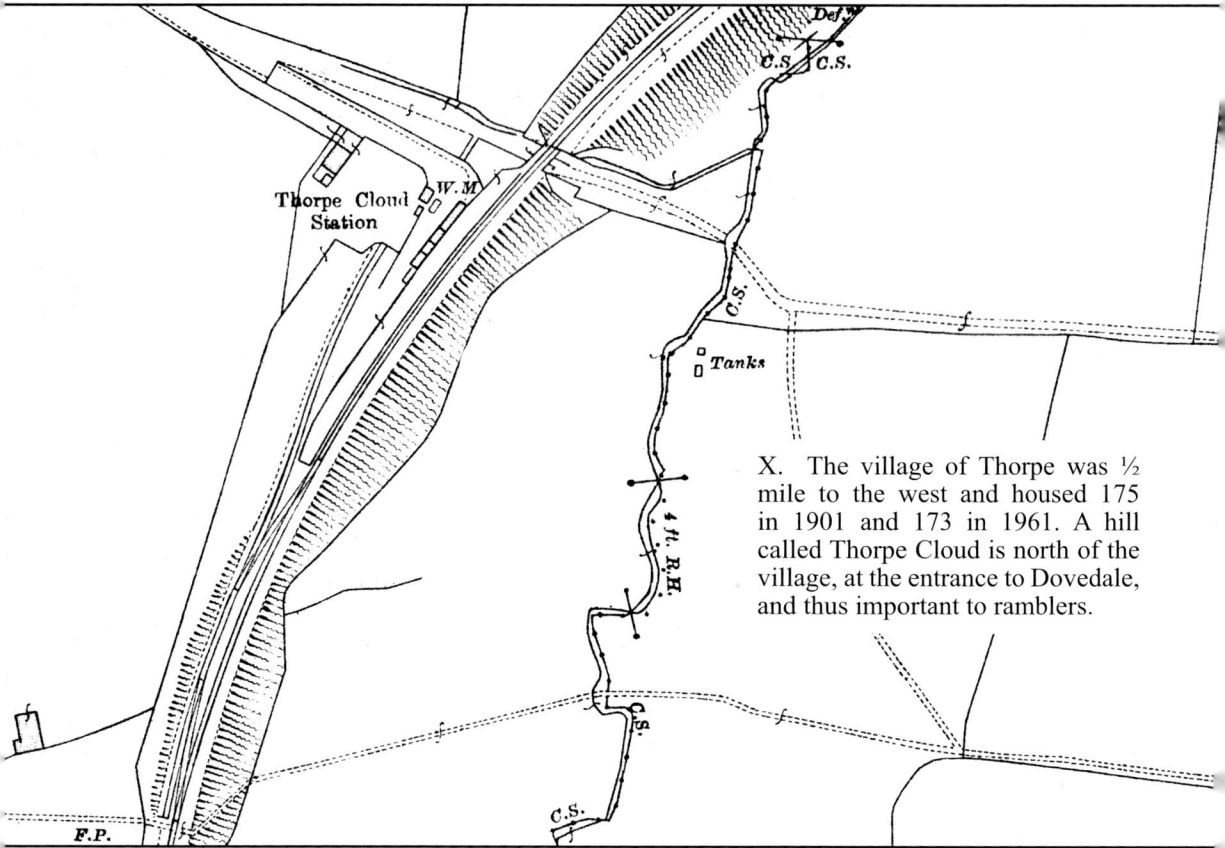

X. The village of Thorpe was ½ mile to the west and housed 175 in 1901 and 173 in 1961. A hill called Thorpe Cloud is north of the village, at the entrance to Dovedale, and thus important to ramblers.

41. A staff of one would normally suffice and an adjacent station master would appear occasionally. The only announcement seen is for the benefit of gentlemen. Just two lamps were needed. (J.Alsop coll.)

42.   Judging by the windows, it is summertime and milk traffic is high. A lightweight platform was built, as it was on the side of a steep valley. Parcels seem plentiful. (P.Laming coll.)

43.   A rough lane and a winding stream pass under the single line, but in reverse order to those shown on the map. The stream flows into Wash Brook. The village starts in the background. (J.Alsop coll.)

44.   Waiting to depart on 9th April 1952 is no. 42605, a 2-6-4T. This 4MT type was introduced by the LMSR in 1935 and was ideal for hilly rural routes, such as this one. The small number on the smoke box is 5F, which means that it was shedded at Uttoxeter. (J.Suter coll.)

45.   We are looking north from a leading compartment on 7th August 1953, with coal travelling at risk. Beyond the fine fence are two coal wagons and a camping coach. The latter were often removed to a depot during the winter, often for maintenance. Most were lost during the 1960s. (H.C.Casserley)

46. Centre in this panorama from May 1959 is the weighing machine office, where road vehicles would be weighed empty and then full. Thus the goods transport could be charged accordingly. (R.Humm coll.)

3rd · SINGLE   SINGLE · 3rd
(No. 2)   (No. 2)
TISSINGTON TO
Tissington   Tissington
Thorpe Cloud   Thorpe Cloud
THORPE CLOUD
(M) 0/4   Fare   0/4 (M)
For conditions see over For conditions see over

1681   1681

L. M. & S. R.
FOR CONDITIONS SEE NOTICES
CHILD
THORPE CLOUD TO
ALSOP-EN-LE-DALE
THIRD
CLASS]   FARE -/4 C

1487   1487

L.M.&S.R.   FOR CONDITIONS SEE BACK
Valid on day of issue only
PARKING TICKET FOR
MOTOR CYCLE
AT
PARSLEY HAY
Registration No...................
Fee -/3 P

T00   T00

3rd-SINGLE   SINGLE-3rd
PARSLEY HAY TO
VIA
HARTINGTON
For alternative routes see book of routes
(M) For conditions see over·   Fare...

041   041

47. A neat garden enhances our long visit. 2-6-4Ts, nos 42609 and 42361, head a 'well dressing' excursion to Tissington on 9th May 1959. (M.J.Stretton coll.)

48. It is 3rd April 1961 and another special train has carried a crowd back home, but from where was not recorded. Mothers stand in the station approach, no doubt sharing the pleasure. (N.D.Mundy)

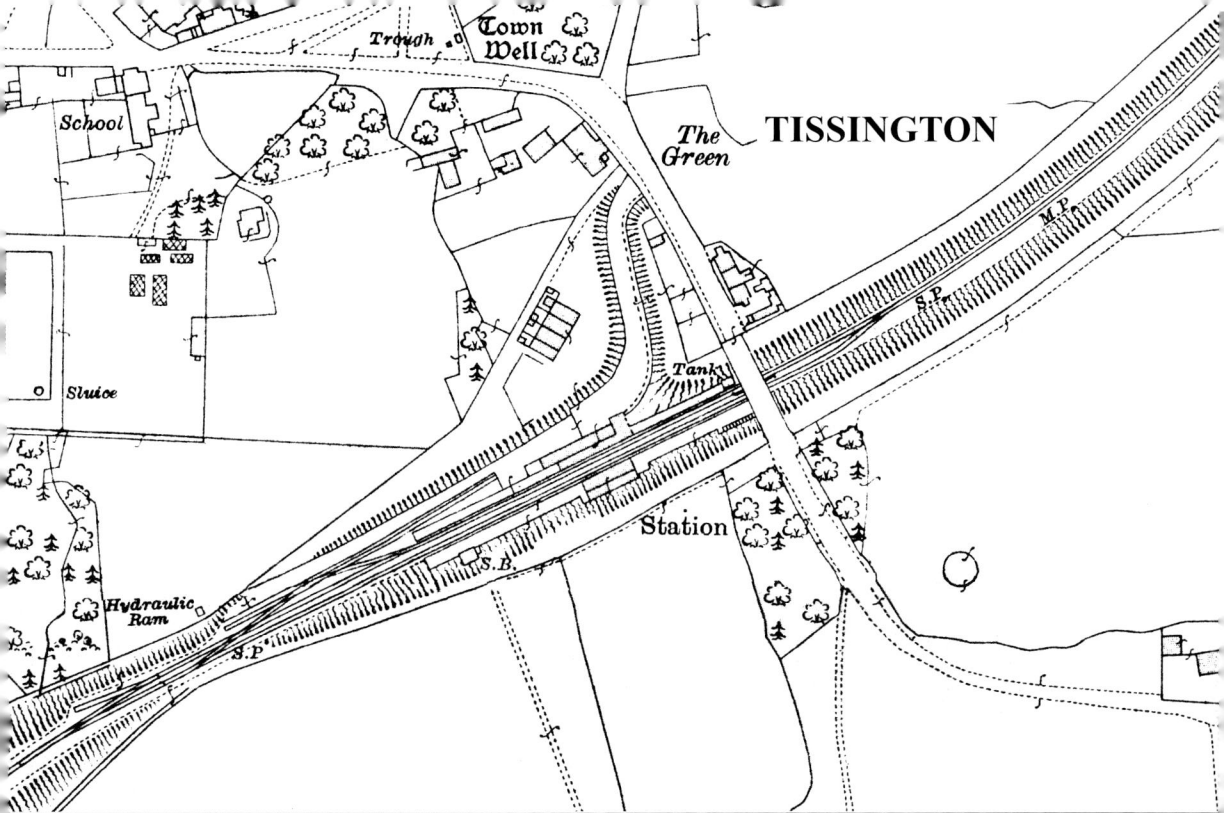

TISSINGTON

XI. The 1922 edition includes the southern part of the village, which housed 363 in 1901 and 173 in 1961. One of the historic wells is indicated, near the top. Well dressing is an ancient Christian custom with its origins lost in time. What is certain is that it is a thanksgiving for a supply of clean water and that it is most prevalent in the Peak District and surrounding area. The dressings themselves are beautifully crafted pictures made from flowers. The event is annual, on Ascension Day, here. The hydraulic ram is a water-powered pump to lift water from a stream. This was probably destined for the tank near the bridge.

49. Clean water for the locomotives was stored in the tank seen at the far end of the down platform. It is shown in this photo from 17th June 1951. An oil lamp can be examined in rare detail. On the left is the parcels shed. (R.Humm coll.)

50.   A train is arriving from Buxton, sometime in the early 1950s. The entire layout was built on the severe gradient of 1 in 60, down from the Peak District. (SLS coll.)

51.   The water column filler hose is hanging at the end of the platform, along with the heating stove, known as a Fire Devil. It is 7th July 1951 and the shrubbery is fine. The goods yard is empty. It was open until 1st November 1954, when regular passenger service ceased on the route. (J.Suter coll.)

52. No. 42366 is piloting no. 42367 with a two-coach special in 1952. The bridge carried a narrow lane which dropped down steeply, after a mile, into the deep valley of the Bradbourne Brook. (R.S.Carpenter coll.)

53. This panorama from 1952 features an unusual request. At least the signalman was told to observe safety procedures. The signal box was in use until 28th February 1959. Crossing behind waiting trains was an important safety measure. (R.S. Carpenter coll.)

54. Showing BRITISH RAILWAYS on 14th April 1952, this 2-6-4T class 4 waits with a long train from Uttoxeter to Buxton, where the engine was based. This is a rare view of the ticket collecting area and the roof over it. It is on the right. (M.J.Stretton coll.)

55. We can examine the up side waiting facility, with its massive chimney. Class 4 2-6-4T no. 42315 is about to depart for Buxton, while a little crowd leaves, on 24th April 1954. (R.J.Buckley/Initial Photographics)

56. The prospective passenger's perspective is seen in October 1954, the month before closure. High standards had been employed by the LNWR in 1899 in terms of the valencing, boarding, kerbing and chimney brickwork. (J.Suter coll.)

57. On the same visit, the goods facilities were recorded, together with the passenger crossing. Seldom were two ground signals in such close proximity. North of here was Fenny Bentley goods siding. It closed on 7th October 1963. (J.Suter coll.)

58.   A retired ex-GWR railcar was a rare visitor in June 1958. There was a total of 38 built between 1934 and 1942. They all had diesel engines; seats ranged from 44 to 104, but only seven had lavatories. (Colour-Rail.com)

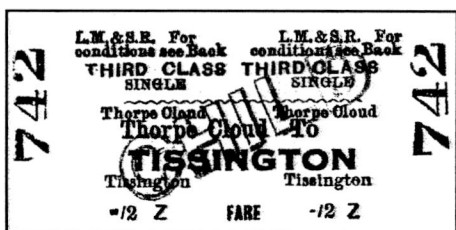

➜   XII. Although almost all trace of the old LNWR lines has disappeared, the trackbed from Ashbourne to Parsley Hay was acquired by Derbyshire County Council and Peak District National Park for a cycle and walking route. The Tissington Trail was one of the first such ventures in the country. It is the vertical section, on the left. Later, Ashbourne Tunnel was acquired by Sustrans. The diagram is from soon after the opening.
(© Peak District National Park Authority)

White Peak Trails and Cycle Routes

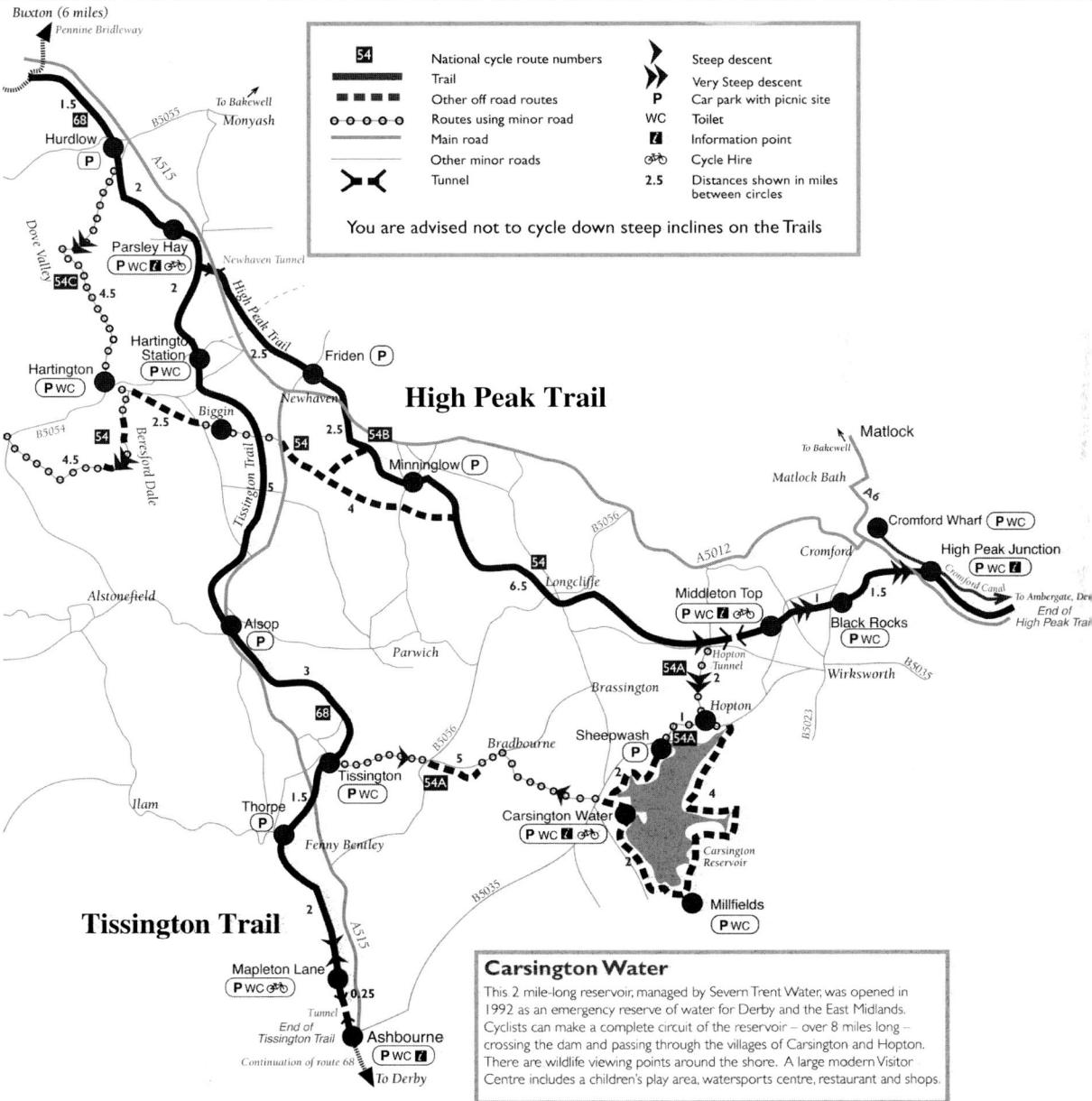

Buxton (6 miles)

Pennine Bridleway

Legend

54	National cycle route numbers	❯	Steep descent
▬▬▬	Trail	❯❯	Very Steep descent
▪ ▪ ▪ ▪	Other off road routes	**P**	Car park with picnic site
○ ○ ○ ○ ○	Routes using minor road	**WC**	Toilet
═══	Main road	ℹ	Information point
—	Other minor roads	🚲	Cycle Hire
✕	Tunnel	**2.5**	Distances shown in miles between circles

You are advised not to cycle down steep inclines on the Trails

To Bakewell · *Monyash*

B5055

1.5 · **68**

Hurdlow · **P**

A515

2

Dove Valley

Parsley Hay · **P WC ℹ 🚲**

Newhaven Tunnel

54C · 4.5 · 2

Hartington Station · **P WC**

High Peak Trail

2.5 · Friden · **P**

High Peak Trail

Hartington · **P WC**

Newhaven

B5054 · **54** · 2.5

Biggin

4.5 · Beresford Dale

Tissington Trail

54 · 2.5 · **54B**

Minninglow · **P**

5

4

54

6.5 · Longcliffe

To Bakewell

Matlock

Matlock Bath

A6

Cromford Wharf · **P WC**

Cromford Canal

High Peak Junction · **P WC ℹ**

To Ambergate, Der
End of High Peak Trail

B5056

A5012

Cromford

Middleton Top · **P WC ℹ 🚲**

1 · 1.5

Black Rocks · **P WC**

Wirksworth

B5023

Alstonefield

Alsop · **P**

Parwich

3

68

Hopton Tunnel

54A · 2

Brassington

B5056

Bradbourne

5

Sheepwash · **P**

54A

Hopton

1

54A

2

4

Ilam

Tissington · **P WC**

54A

1.5

Thorpe · **P**

Fenny Bentley

Carsington Water · **P WC ℹ 🚲**

2

Carsington Reservoir

2

Millfields · **P WC**

B5035

Tissington Trail

A515

2

Mapleton Lane · **P WC 🚲**

0.25

Tunnel
End of Tissington Trail

Ashbourne · **P WC ℹ**

Continuation of route 68

To Derby

Carsington Water

This 2 mile-long reservoir, managed by Severn Trent Water, was opened in 1992 as an emergency reserve of water for Derby and the East Midlands. Cyclists can make a complete circuit of the reservoir – over 8 miles long – crossing the dam and passing through the villages of Carsington and Hopton. There are wildlife viewing points around the shore. A large modern Visitor Centre includes a children's play area, watersports centre, restaurant and shops.

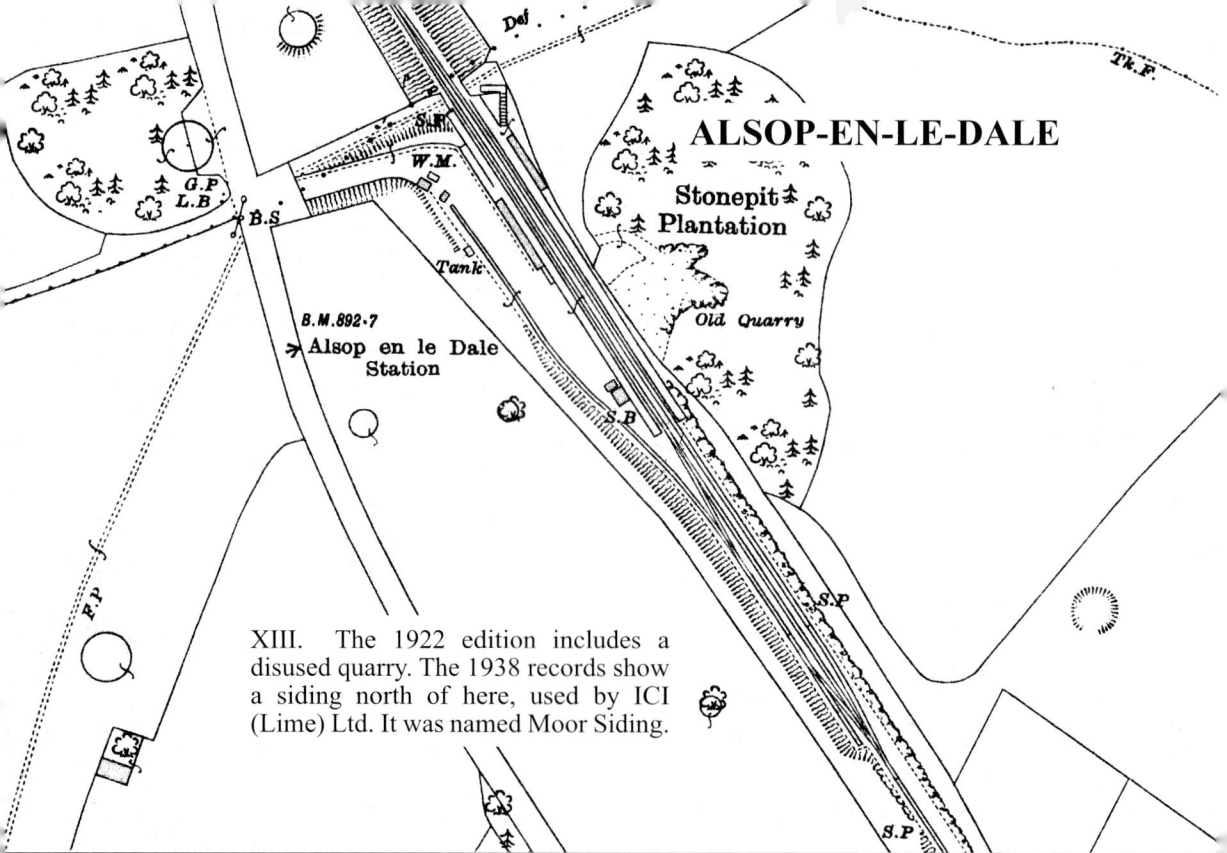

ALSOP-EN-LE-DALE

Stonepit
Plantation

Old Quarry

Alsop en le Dale
Station

B.M.892·7

XIII. The 1922 edition includes a disused quarry. The 1938 records show a siding north of here, used by ICI (Lime) Ltd. It was named Moor Siding.

59. This is the down platform soon after its opening. The station master is near slotted boxes of a type often used for vegetables. Similar sized baskets were used for pullets and racing pigeons. (J.Alsop coll.)

60. The bridge carries the A515, which received its number in 1919, after so many army lorries came into commercial use. The up starting signal was of LNWR design. Another 1952 view follows. (R.S.Carpenter)

61. Lack of an entrance in this elevation was due to the sloping ground. The high level door was used for parcel room access. (R.S.Carpenter)

62. The 10.10 Uttoxeter to Buxton is seen on 7th August 1953, hauled by 2-6-4T no. 42368. Access to the up platform is between the running-in board and the end of the building. (H.C.Casserley)

63. It is 4th September 1954 and 2-6-4T no. 42590 is running in with a Uttoxeter-Buxton service, close to smart new ballasting. (J.Suter coll.)

64. This and the next picture are from October 1954. Below the complex bridge structure in the foreground is a footpath. The LNWR cared for safety and was also generous, usually. (J.Suter coll.)

65. The main road crosses the left skyline as rain covers the platforms entirely. Avoidance of canopies was an unexpected LNWR economy measure. Even the chimneys are short, to save money. (J.Suter coll.)

66. Goods stock abounds in June 1955, as two 0-8-0s were passing. The home signal is behind the hard-working loco on the right. The 1 in 71 climb eased to 1 in 260 through the station. The view is from the signal box. (R.S.Carpenter coll.)

67.   The regular crossing was photographed again on 16th November 1961, but at the other end of the station. The station approach is on the right. The telephone system was obviously minimal. Nottingham High School used the station shortly after its closure as a geography field centre, using the station buildings as accommodation for the students. (SLS coll.)

68.   The signal box is seen in May 1962. It had 25 levers and closed on 7th October 1963, as did the goods yard. Nearby is the operator's Ford 8. The track was lifted in 1964, despite new materials being evident. (M.J.Stretton coll.)

HARTINGTON

Old Limekiln

B.M. 1037·1

G.P.

Old Limekiln

Station Quarry

S.P.

F.W.

B.M. 984·9

Def.

F.W.

Hand Dale Farm

S.P.

S.P.

P

W.M.

Hartington Station

S.B.

Goods Shed

Cr.

F.P.

S.P.

F.P.

F.P.

F.B.

S.P.

S.P.

L. & N.W.R.
ASHBOURNE & BUXTON

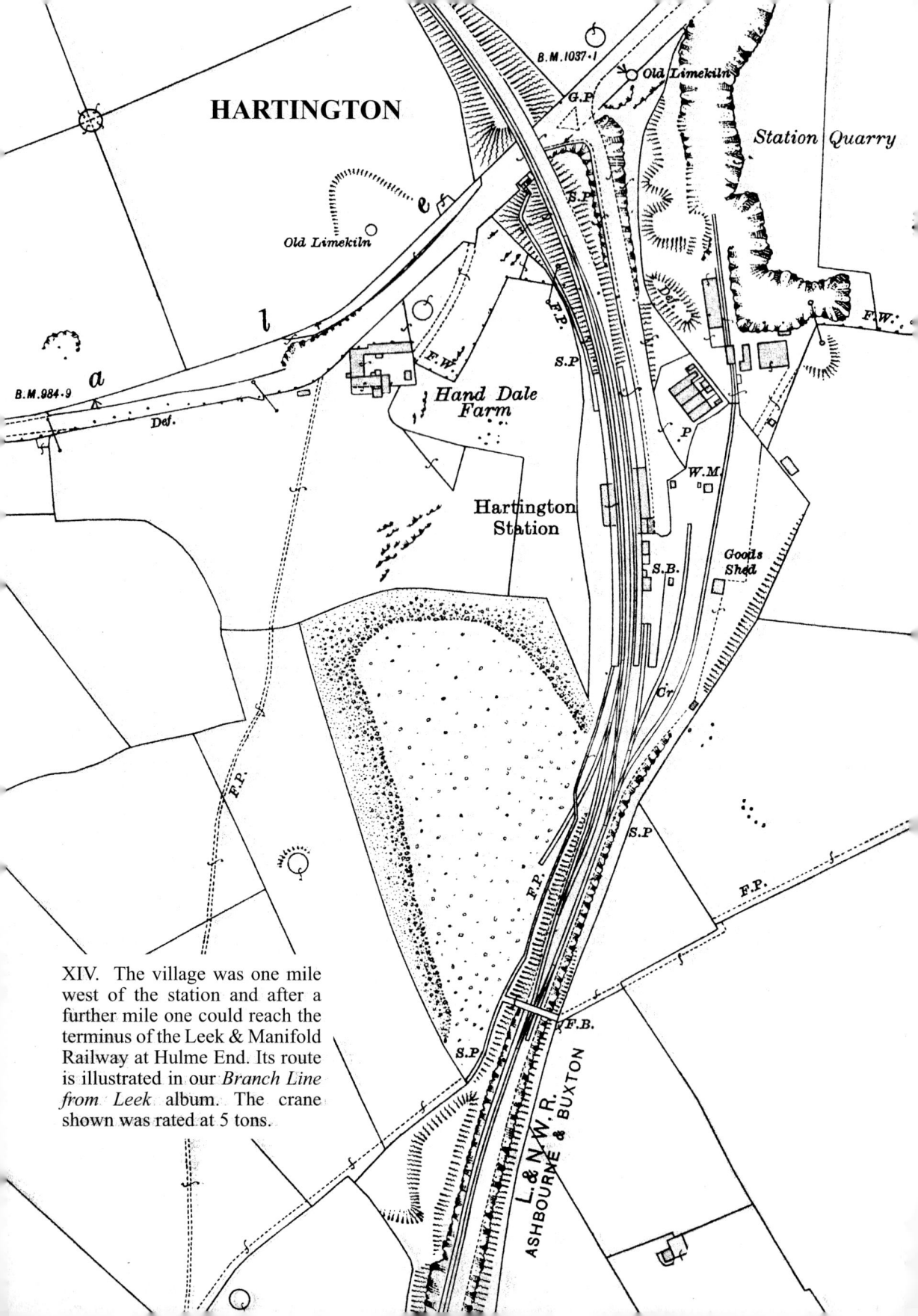

XIV. The village was one mile west of the station and after a further mile one could reach the terminus of the Leek & Manifold Railway at Hulme End. Its route is illustrated in our *Branch Line from Leek* album. The crane shown was rated at 5 tons.

69. The up side is seen in May 1953, while box repairs proceed. Built on a severe slope at just over 1000ft above sea level, problems were anticipated by providing wooden platforms of light weight. (J.Alsop coll.)

← 69a. The signal box and many of its levers have been preserved. The box is near Hartington station car park, which gives direct access to the Tissington Trail.
(© Peak District National Park Authority)

70. The running-in board is seen on 7th August 1953, when it would serve for a further 15 months until its closure in November 1954. The climate is challenging at this height. (H.C.Casserley)

↑ 71. As there was no footbridge, passengers had to use the barrow crossing. Water for both the station and the nearby Hartington Quarry was brought by rail, using a tender. It is 3rd August 1959 and decay is starting. In the foreground is the end loading dock. (R.Humm coll.)

72. We pass through on 11th May 1963 on an RCTS Tour. The train started at St Pancras and ran via Derby to Buxton. It is on its return, which was via Kettering to London. The locomotive here is no. 61004 *Oryx*, a class B1 4-6-0. (R.Humm coll.)

73. This is the scene in 1967. Goods traffic had ceased on 6th July 1964. The station buildings were demolished long after closure, but the typical LNWR signal box has been preserved as a visitor centre. It had 20 levers and was closed on 25th October 1967. Quarry trains continued from the north until that time. (A.F.Bullimore)

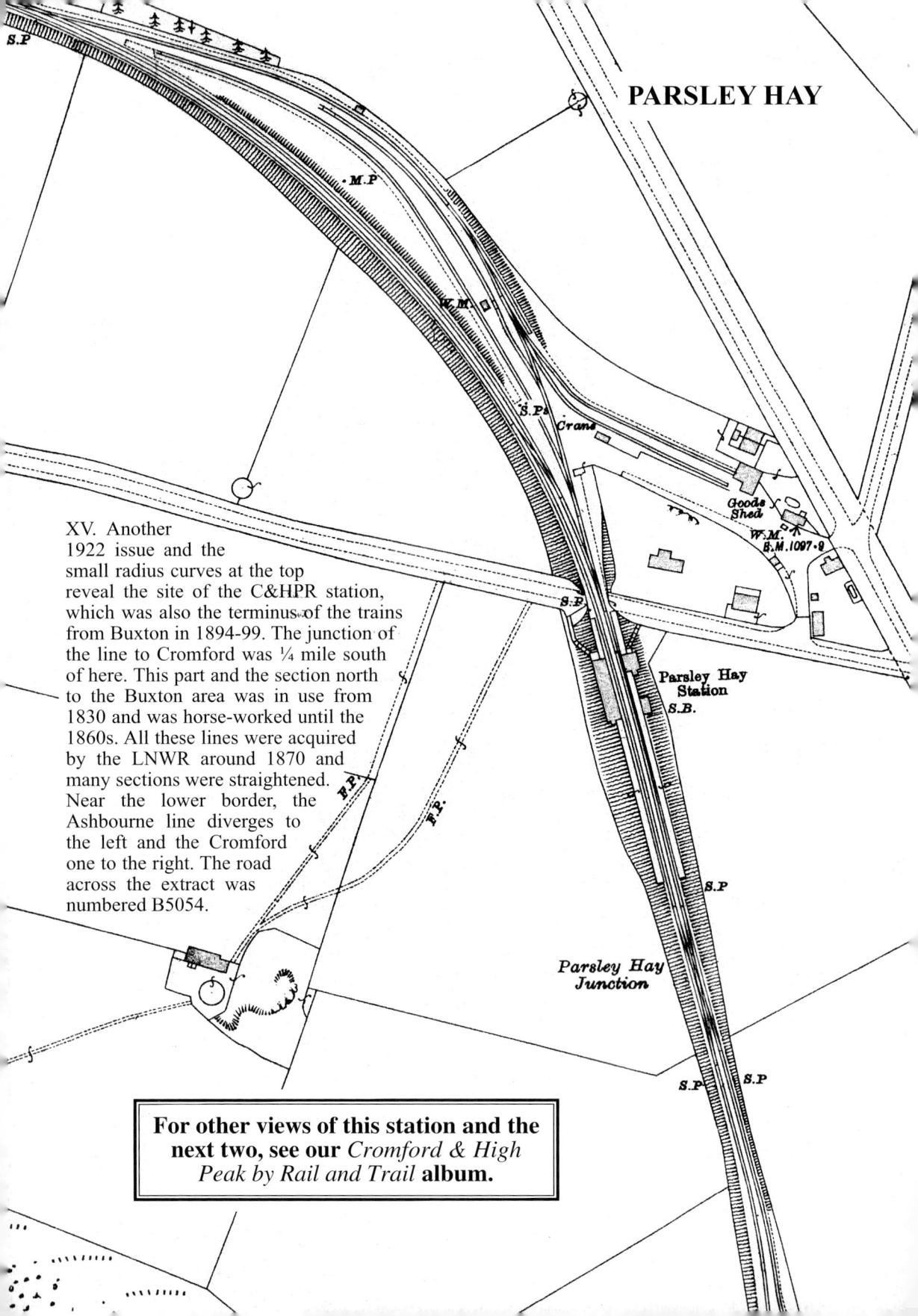

PARSLEY HAY

S.P

.M.P

W.M

S.P

Crane

W.M
B.M.1097·9

Goods
Shed

S.P

XV. Another
1922 issue and the
small radius curves at the top
reveal the site of the C&HPR station,
which was also the terminus of the trains
from Buxton in 1894-99. The junction of
the line to Cromford was ¼ mile south
of here. This part and the section north
to the Buxton area was in use from
1830 and was horse-worked until the
1860s. All these lines were acquired
by the LNWR around 1870 and
many sections were straightened.
Near the lower border, the
Ashbourne line diverges to
the left and the Cromford
one to the right. The road
across the extract was
numbered B5054.

Parsley Hay
Station
S.B.

F.P.

F.P.

S.P

Parsley Hay
Junction

S.P

S.P   S.P

For other views of this station and the
next two, see our *Cromford & High
Peak by Rail and Trail* album.

74.   A view south in May 1950 confirms that we have reached the Peak District. We are almost 1100ft above sea level. There are very few dwellings nearby; the station was named after a farm. (J.Alsop coll.)

75.   We look south to see Parsley Hay Junction and the single line to Cromford on the left, plus the one to Hartington curving on the right. (R.S.Carpenter coll.)

76. Now we witness a train arriving from Buxton, but sadly devoid of details. We can admire the weather protection over both platforms and the panels for the benefit of gentlemen, on the left. (W.A.Camwell/SLS coll.)

77. Again without any data, we can witness a special running in from the north. It is waiting at the home signal, probably for the crossover to be switched. The full extent of the goods yard runs to the left border. It closed on 6th June 1964. (R.Humm coll.)

↑ 78. The date is 7th April 1959 and here is evidence of important track work in progress nearby. On the right are two Drewry railcars with central engines, above which sat two rows of gangers. On the left is no. 12006 of class D3/7, an ex-LMS 0-6-0 diesel shunter. Thirty were built in 1939-42. (J.Suter coll.)

79. Running from Buxton on 15th April 1961 are two 2-car DMUs. Level with their front is the 5-ton crane. This train is described in caption 40. It is running towards Parsley Hay Junction, having reversed on the triangle at Buxton. (Colour-Rail.com)

MANCHESTER, NEW MILLS, WHALEY BRIDGE, BUXTON, and ASHBOURNE.—L. & N. W.

Miles	Up.						Week Days.											
	London Road Station,	mrn	mrn	mrn	mrn	mrn	aft	aft	aft	aft	aft	aft		aft	aft		aft	aft	aft
	Manchester ....dep.	7 35	S 40	9 17		1135	12 5	1220	1250	1255	1 5		1 20	2 25		3 40	4 5	4 50
518	Liverpool (Lime St) dep.		6 5			9 25	9 55						1220			1215	3 35	
484	Chester (Gen.) 518 ″	2 7	6/45		9 53	1023			1130			1145	1229		2 15		
504	Crewe ″	4c35	7 25	8 5	1035	1115	1148	1148	1210		1248	1 42	3 10	4 0	
510	Macclesfield * ″	6 30	8 20	9 5	1045	1138		1230				2 2	2 57	4 13	
5½	Stockport ....dep.	7 47	9 0	9 27	1155	1215	1235	1 0	9 15	1 31	1 37	2 35	3 50	4 15	4 59
7½	Davenport	7 53	9 4		12 0	1239		1 31	22		1 41	2 41	3 55	4 21	
8½	Hazel Grove	7 57	9 8		12 4	1243		1 18	1 26		1 45	2 45	3 58	4 25	
—	677 Macclesfield (Cen.) dep.	7 58		9 0	1048		1228		1228					3 58	
	Bollington	7 45		9 7	1055		1235		1235				2 32		4 5
10½	Middlewood, for High Lane	8 4	9 13	9 30	1210		1248		1 24		1 50	2 51		4 31
12½	Disley .... (677	8 9	9 18	9 45	1216		1250	1253	1 29		1 45	1 55	2 57	4 6	4 37
14	New Mills 676	8 12	9 21	9 48	1220		1234	1256			1 49	1 59	3 1		4 41
15½	Furness Vale	8 18	9 25		1224		1 0					2 43	6		4 46
16½	Whaley Bridge	8 22	9 29	9 55	1228		1240	1 4			1 55	2 7	3 10	4 13	4 49
20½	Chapel-en-le-Frith :	8 33		10 6		1250		1 26			2 4		3 20	4 23	4 59	5 28
22½	Dove Holes	8 40		1012		1257		1 31			2 11		3 28		5 6
25	Fairfield, for Golf Links ½			1017			1 2		1 37		2 17			4 32		5 37
25½	Buxton 573, 573 ... { arr.	8 49		1020		1 5		1 40		2 20		3 39		4 35	5 15	5 40
	.... { dep.	7 35	9 0	1020		1245				2 57					5 55
26	Higher Buxton		9 3	1023						2 30					5 58
29	Hindlow	7 45	9 12	1042						2 39					6 5
32½	Hurdlow	7 53	9 18	1048						2 45					6 11
34½	Parsley Hay	7 58	9 26	1057						2 54					6 16
36½	Hartington	8 2	9 32	11 4		1 7				3 0					6 21
41	Alsop-en-le-Dale, for Dove-	8 11	9 40	1113		1 16				3 8					6 31
43½	Tissington	8 22	9 45	1121		1 21				3 15					6 45
46	Thorpe Cloud, for Dovedale	8 29	9 49	1125		1 24				3 19					6 53
48	Ashbourne 544 ......arr.	8 32	9 54	1130		1 31				3 25					7 2

Timetable for October 1912, continued opposite.

80. Admirers gaze on as an RCTS Sheffield Branch Railtour waits on 27th June 1964. It was hauled by no. 61360, an Eastern Region class B1 4-6-0. The fare was 30 shillings. (T.Owen/Colour-Rail.com)

up.		Week Days—Continued.													Sundays.			
London Road Station.		aft	aft	aft	aft	aft	aft	aft	aft	aft	aft	aft	aft		mrn	aft	aft	aft
Manchester ....dep.		4 50	5 12	5 20	5 40	6	0	6 22	6 22	6 50	7 30	8 40	9 30	1025	1115	9 20	2 0	....	6 9
518 Liverpool (LimeSt.)dep.		3 35	3 35	....	4 20	....	....	....	5 10	5	....	8 35	....	....	....	....	7 35	....	2 10
484 Chester (Gen.) 518 ,,		....	....	....	4 20	5	0 5	0	....	6 20	7 15	7 40	....	....	....	2	7 ...	....	3 45
504 Crewe ..... ,,		4 0	4 33	4 39	....	5 10	5 38	5 38	6 25	6 40	7 30	8 10	9 50	1024	....	....	5 30	....	5 10
510 Macclesfield * . .. ,,		4 13	4 13	4 50	4 50	5 45	6 13	....	6/45	7 55	....	9 20	1020	....	7	5 9	30	....	5 10
Stockport ....dep.		5	5 5	5 22	5 30	6 10	6 32	6 37	7	0 7	43	8 50	9 44	1035	1125	9 30	2 21	....	6 22
Davenport .... ,,		5	9 Sat. 5 36		6 16	....	6 43	7	6	7 47	8 57	....	9 48	1041	1131	....	9 37	2 28	....	6 28
Hazel Grove........ ,,		5 13	Sat. 5 41		6 21	....	6 48	7	10	7 52	9	1	9 53	1045	1139	....	9 41	2 32	....	6 32
677 Macclesfield (Gen.) dep.		....	....	....	....	....	7	18	....	....	....	....	....	....	....	....	....	....	
Bollington ...... ,,		....	....	....	6	7	....	7	25	....	....	....	....	....	....	....	....	....	
Middlewood, for High Lane		....	5 47	....	6 27	6 54	7 16	7 58	9	8 10	1051	....	....	....	....	....	....	
Disley............ {677}		5 36	....	6 33	6 46	7	0	7 21	8	3 9	1410	6	1056	1148	....	9 50	2 41	....	6 41
New Mills 676.......		5 41	....	6 38	....	7	2	8 7	9 17	10	1059	1151	....	....	9 55	2 44	....	6 44
Furness Vale........		5 44	....	6 42	....	7	29	8 11	9 23	10	1311	3	Sat.	....	9 59	....	....	6 52
Whaley Bridge......		5 47	....	6 45	6 53	7	32	8 14	9 26	10 16	11	6	1159	....	....	10	2 50	....	6 55
Chapel-en-le-Frith ⁑		5 57	....	6 53	6 7	4	3	7 43	....	9 37	1027	1117	12	9	....	1013	3	....	7	5
Dove Holes		6	4	....	7	8	4 7	18	7 51	....	9 45	10/35	....	Sat.	....	1021	3	8	....	7 13
Fairfield, for Golf Links ⁑		....	**b**	....	....	....	....	....	....	....	....	....	....	....	....	....	....	
Buxton 573, 578 { arr. { dep.		6 12	....	6 25	7 18	....	7 58	....	9 55	10/45	1130	1224	....	1035	15	....	7 25
																....	5	6	
Higher Buxton																....	5 10		
Hindlow...........																....	5 17		
Hurdlow...........																....	5 22		
Parsley Hay........																....	5 29		
Hartington ....{dale}																....	5 39		
Alsop-en-le-Dale, for Dove-																....	5 51		
Tissington																6	6		
Thorpe Cloud, for Dovedale																6	8		
Ashbourne 544... arr.																6 15		

For Local Trains and Intermediate Stations
BETWEEN PAGE
Manchester and **Stockport**...................502
Macclesfield & Bollington.......................677

a Sets down on Tuesdays and Fridays on informing Guard at Stockport.   **b** Stops to set down on informing the Guard at Manchester.   *c* Leaves at 5 mrn. on Mondays.   *d* Except Tuesdays and Thursdays.   *g* Except Mondays.   *h* Leaves at 6 13 aft. on Saturdays.   *k* Via Manchester.   *s* Saturdays only.   * Hibel Road Station.   ⁑ Over 1 mile to the Midland Station.   ‖ Alighting Platform only.

81. Here is our first view of one of the two stairways down to the road, plus the usual barrow crossing. We have a 'Lion and Monocycle' on the tender and a motorcycle and sidecar on the platform. (R.Humm coll.)

82. Ex-LMS class 2MT 2-6-0 no. 46492 creeps past on 13th May 1967. The line from Hartington north to Hindlow closed on 25th October 1967, as did the signal box. It had opened in 1894 with a 20-lever frame, which was later extended to 36. (Colour-Rail.com)

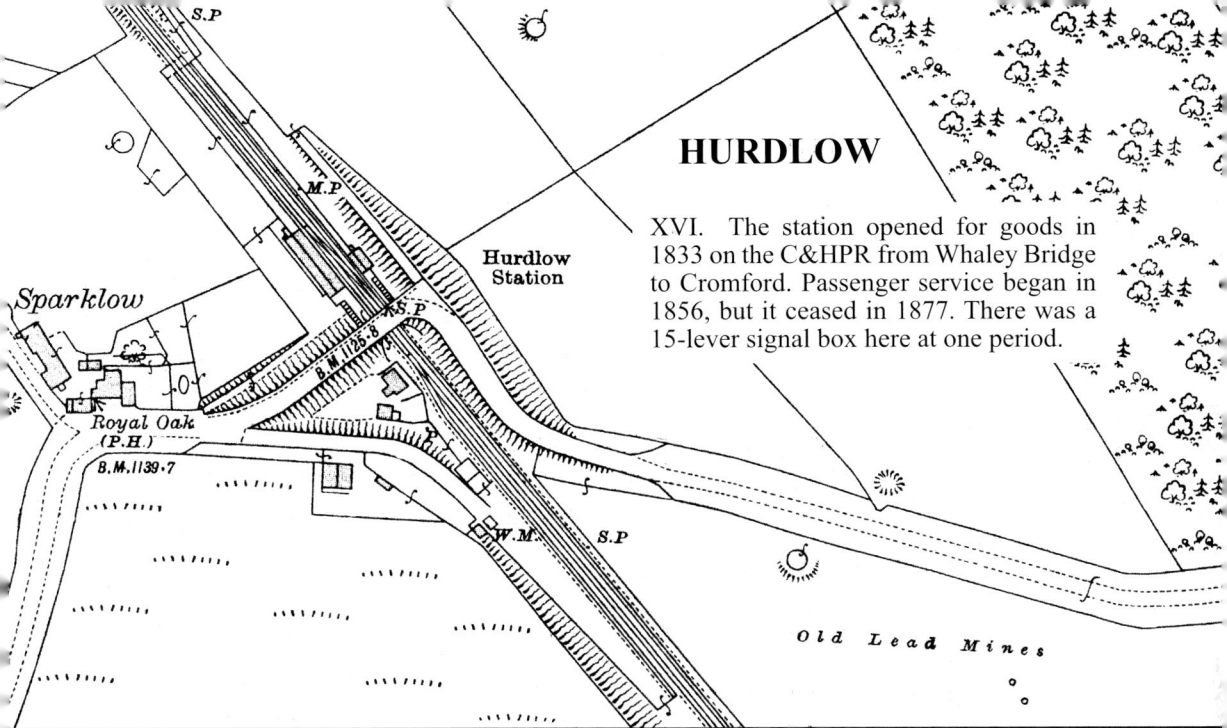

HURDLOW

XVI. The station opened for goods in 1833 on the C&HPR from Whaley Bridge to Cromford. Passenger service began in 1856, but it ceased in 1877. There was a 15-lever signal box here at one period.

↑ 83. The station was opened again on 4th August 1899. This view is towards Parsley Hay in May 1953. The community was so small that it did not have a census heading. It was named on the 1 in scale map (no. XVII); three houses are shown. (J.Alsop coll.)

84. Easter Tuesdays were particularly busy with special trains laid on for the Flagg Moor Steeplechase. The station closed on 15th August 1949, along with the goods yard. Only the loading gauge and cattle pen remained. This picture is from 25th October 1954 and shows 2-6-4T no. 42365 with the 11.40am from Uttoxeter. (J.Suter coll.)

DOWLOW HALT

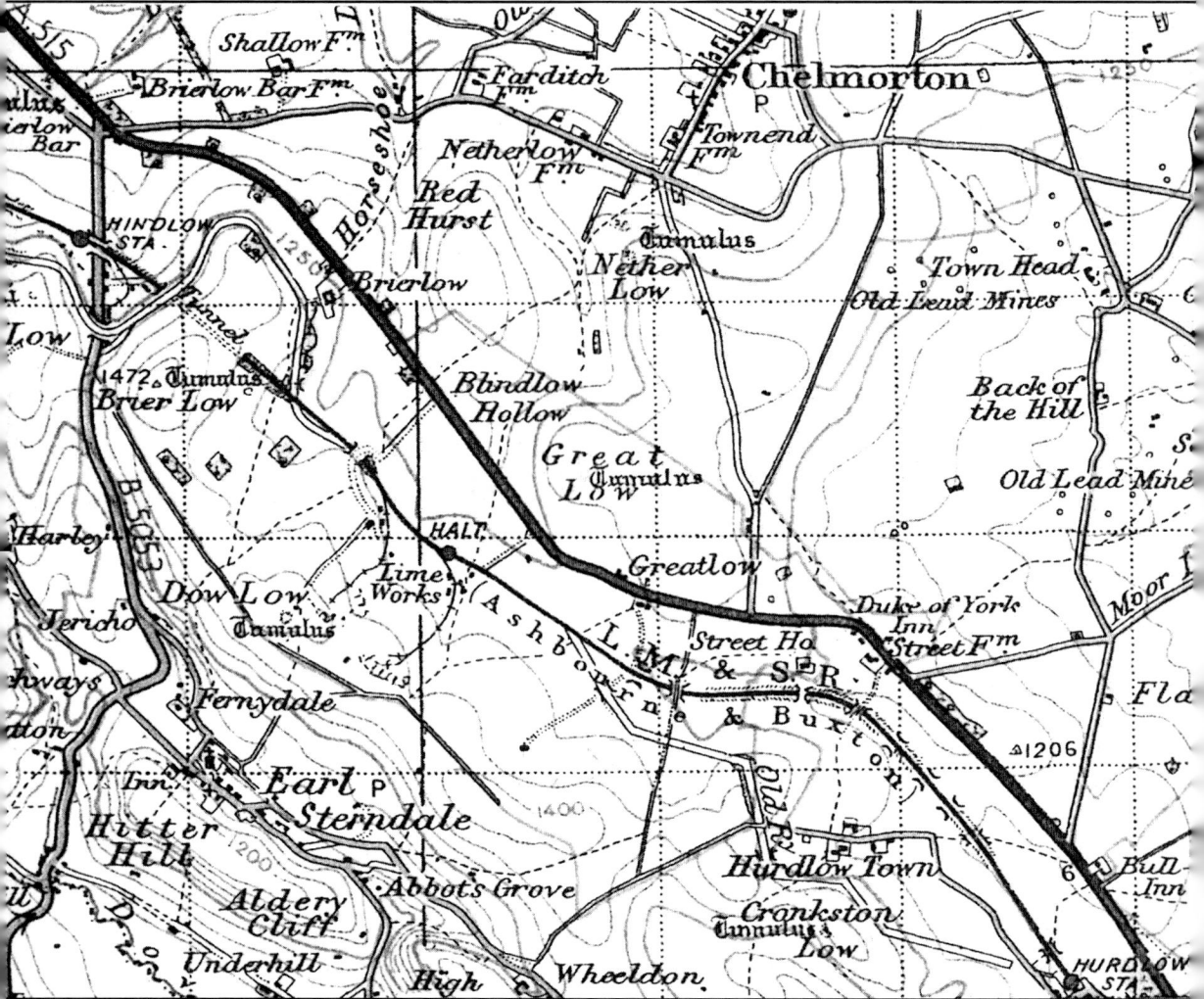

XVII. The 1947 edition is shown at 2ins to 1 mile with the halt left of centre, together with two curves to Briggs Sidings nearby. The adjacent stations are also included and track diversions are detailed in the caption for the next map. Briggs Sidings served Messrs Briggs and the Dowlow Lime & Stone Company, later Steetley, and then Redland Aggregates. In 2019, the line from the north was still serving Buxton Lime Industries, also terminating a short distance further east at the Lafarge Dowlow sidings.

London & North Western Rv.
Issued subject to the conditions & regulations in the Cos Time Tables Books Bills & Notices.

HURDLOW TO
BUXTON(L&NW)

Third}   1042(S.)   [Class
           BUXTON   FARE -/7

27MY.99

3192

85. This is the summit of our journey at 1260ft. The halt was built in 1920 for use by workmen at the quarries. It was open to the public from 4th November 1929 to 1st November 1954. Workers continued to use it for an unknown time. (W.A.Camwell/SLS)

86. Briggs Siding Box was opened in June 1894 with 18 levers. It had 21 when the line was singled to Parsley Hay and was closed on 18th May 1969. (A.F.Bullimore)

HINDLOW

XVIII. Hindlow Tunnel was 514 yds long and begins at the right border of this 1922 map. Crossing it there are the earthworks of the C&HPR, which carried rails from 1831 until 1892. Its complete course is on map XVII and was almost level. It is in two parts, each side of the halt and is annotated above the words Hurdlow Town.

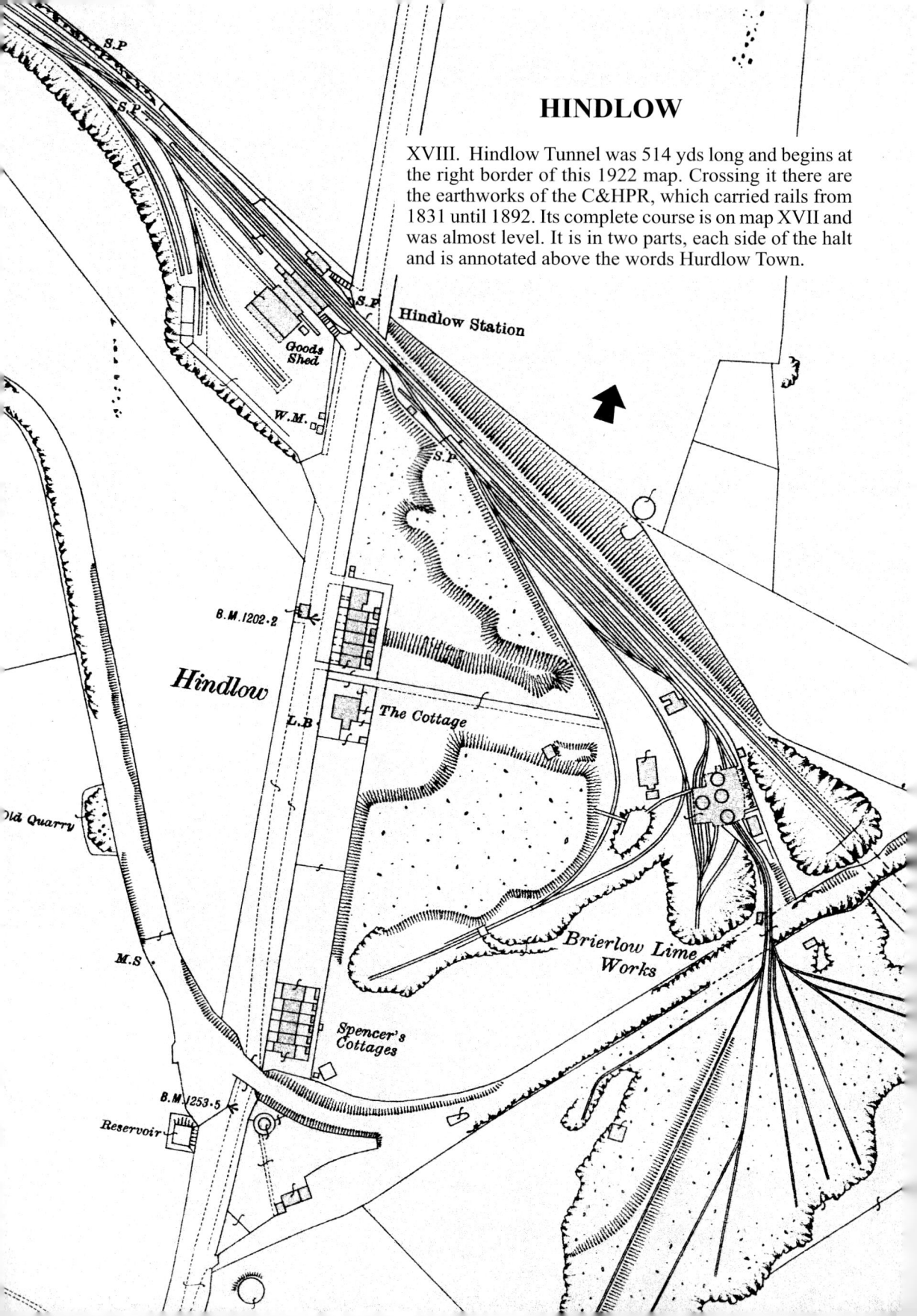

S.P

S.P

S.P Hindlow Station

Goods Shed

W.M.

S.P

B.M.1202·2

Hindlow

L.B.

The Cottage

Old Quarry

M.S

Brierlow Lime Works

Spencer's Cottages

B.M.1253·5

Reservoir

87. It is 17th May 1953 and the need for Hindlow Tunnel becomes clear. Lime kilns are evident to the right of it. Two small chimneys on the extreme right show the need for extra water heating at this altitude. (R.S.Carpenter coll.)

88. Seldom seen are the cords and levers above the tank which controlled the valves. Working the Manchester Locomotive Society 'High Peak Rail Tour' on 25th April 1953 is 0-6-0 3F no. 43618. The train had visited Middleton Top and was now bound for Buxton. (J.Suter coll.)

89. Departing on 25th October 1954 is the 11.40 Uttoxeter to Buxton usual two-coach train. A worn path shows that the parcel doors had been used sometimes. Picture 91 shows the developments that took place here later. (J.Suter coll.)

90. The WAY OUT could still be found on 4th May 1957. It was down the stairs. Working mineral empties is 8F 2-8-0 no. 48740. It was based at shed 9D, which was Buxton. The station was demolished in 1966. (R.Humm coll.)

91.   Two panoramas from 1st June 1962 contain extensive limestone workings relating to 1892 railway development. The foreground contains a recent shed and sidings. Improvements for storage of sacks of grain had been a recent requirement. (J.Suter coll.)

92.   The signal box was just beyond the upper border of the map. It had opened in 1894 with 27 levers. Ten more were added when the line to Parsley Hay was singled. Closure came in 1982. There were sidings for Ryan, Somerville & Company, and another for W.Spencer & Company (later Buxton Lime Firms Ltd). These were two of the many lime works served by this stretch of line. (J.Suter coll.)

93. In 2019, the line was still open from Buxton to Hindlow for stone traffic from Buxton Lime Industries and Lafarge Dowlow. Nos 20041 and 20307 approach Briggs Sidings ground frame with three wagonloads of lime from Dowlow on 28th August 1986. This was the 13.20 trip working from Dowlow to Peak Forest, from where the wagons would continue on a Speedlink train to Warrington and then on further trains to either Barnby Dun or Mossend. (P.D.Shannon)

94. After quarrying ceased at Hindlow, the adjacent lime works received its stone from Tunstead. BR began running regular trains from Tunstead to Hindlow in January 1988. The trains used spare ICI vacuum-braked hopper wagons from the fleet that served Lostock and Oakleigh works near Northwich. Nos 37679 and 37683 have just arrived at Hindlow with the 09.15 train from Tunstead on 9th April 1988. (P.D.Shannon)

95. The Tunstead-Hindlow trains went over to air-braked operation in the early 1990s, using hired wagons and class 60 haulage. No. 60085 sets back past Briggs Sidings ground frame into the terminal at Hindlow with stone from Tunstead on 22nd July 1994. On the left is a rake of two-axle hopper wagons awaiting reloading at Dowlow. (P.D.Shannon)

NORTH OF HINDLOW

96. Shortly after leaving Buxton, trains passed over this impressive structure created by the LNWR on a new route to avoid a winding part of the C&HPR. We witness no. 40135 hauling a mineral train on 17th September 1980. (T.Heavyside)

97. Dukes Drive Viaduct passes over a stream and a lane about ½ mile south of Higher Buxton. It has 13 arches; eight are shown above. Seen in June 1953 is no. 42440, an ex-LMS 2-6-4T, leaving the structure. (J.Suter coll.)

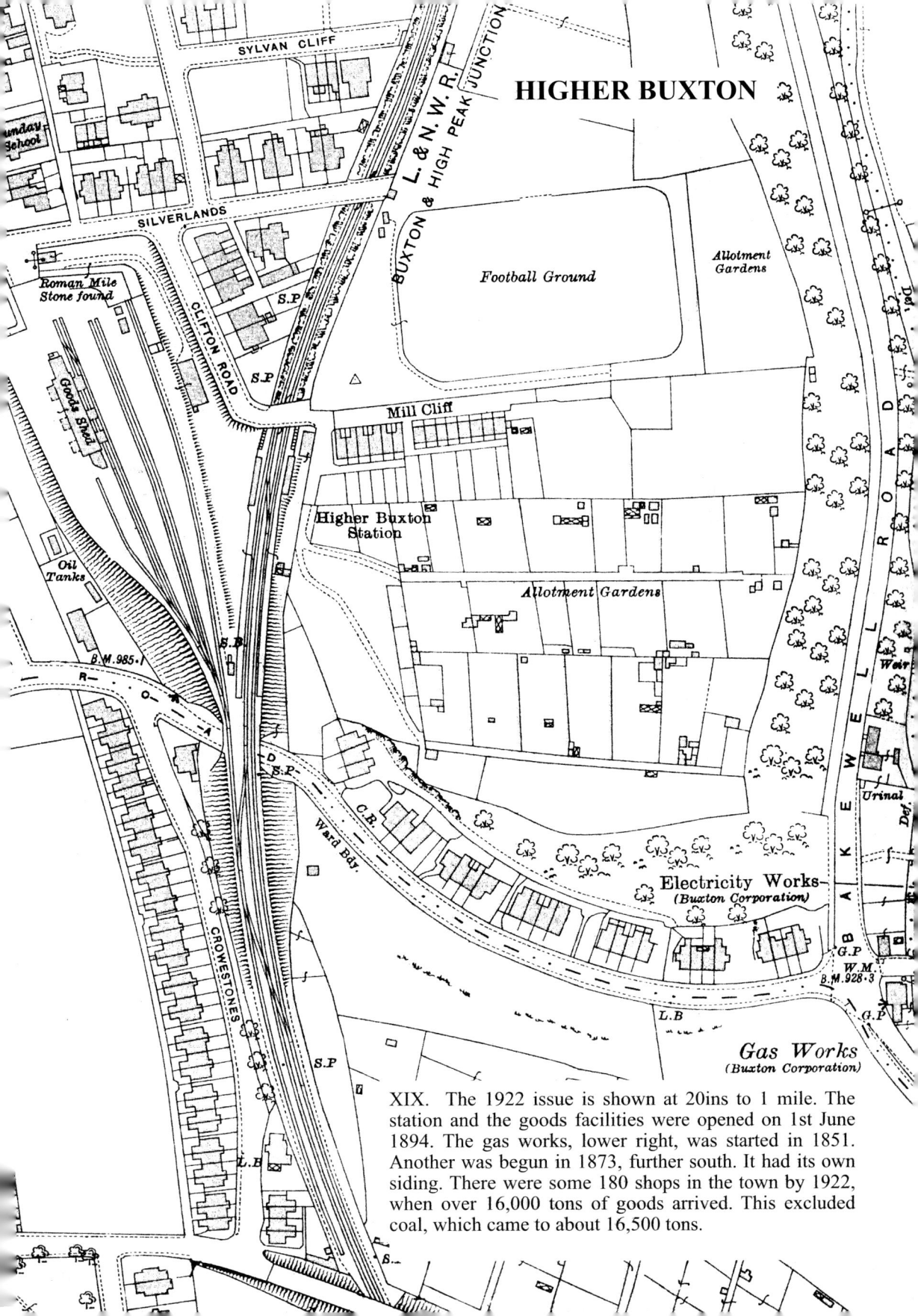

HIGHER BUXTON

SYLVAN CLIFF

SILVERLANDS

L. & N. W. R.

BUXTON & HIGH PEAK JUNCTION

Football Ground

Allotment Gardens

Roman Mile Stone found

CLIFTON ROAD

S.P.

S.P.

Goods Shed

Mill Cliff

△

Higher Buxton Station

Oil Tanks

Allotment Gardens

B.M.985.1

S.B.

R——O——A——D

S.P.

Ward Bdy.

C.B.

CROWESTONES

B A K E W E L L   R O A D

Bdy.

Weir

Urinal

Electricity Works
(Buxton Corporation)

G.P.
W.M.
B.M.928.3

L.B.

G.P.

L.B.

S.P.

S.P.

S.P.

L.B.

Gas Works
(Buxton Corporation)

XIX. The 1922 issue is shown at 20ins to 1 mile. The
station and the goods facilities were opened on 1st June
1894. The gas works, lower right, was started in 1851.
Another was begun in 1873, further south. It had its own
siding. There were some 180 shops in the town by 1922,
when over 16,000 tons of goods arrived. This excluded
coal, which came to about 16,500 tons.

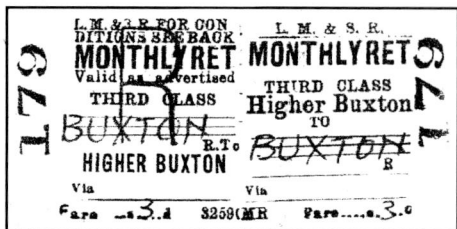

98. It is June 1930 and ex-LNWR 0-6-2T no. 6899 is working the 1.45pm to Ashbourne. Washing is being dried in the garden on the right; it is not a photographic fault. (J.Suter coll.)

99. The station is seen in LMS days, with its direct accesses to Clifton Road. Closure to passengers came on 2nd April 1951. The bridge in the background gave access to only the football ground. (Stations UK)

100. The link to the goods yard is on the right of this panorama from the road bridge on 21st June 1969, when the track was being simplified. Only a few wooden posts remain as evidence of the station. The signal box had 20 levers and opened with the line, closing on 18th May 1969.
(Milepost 92½)

101. The skew arch is on a gradient of 1 in 62 and is seen again in the next picture. We are lower right on the next map and watch a Buxton to Ashbourne service pass over the ex-MR tracks on 10th May 1951. It is worked by no. 42461, a class 4 2-6-4T. (J.Suter coll.)

102. The bridge under the fifth coach is the one featured in the previous view. We witness a special arriving from Ashbourne on 12th September 1954. A loading gauge is unclear on the right. (J.Suter coll.)

103. Approaching the town on 14th August 1958 is no. 43300, a class 3F 0-6-0. This type numbered 319 in 1948 and had been introduced by the MR in 1885. The nearest car is a Standard 14. (J.Suter coll.)

1148 British Rlys(M) For conditions see back Third Class Single — British Rlys(M) For conditions see back Third Class Single 1148

Hindlow — Hindlow

Hindlow To

DOWLOW

Dowlow — Dowlow

-/3½ Z FARE -/3½ Z

026 L.M.& S.R. For conditions see notices. MONTHLYRET Valid as advertised THIRD CLASS Hartington TO HIGHER BUXTON Fare 2/3C — L.M.& S.R. MONTHLYRET THIRD CLASS Higher Buxton TO HARTINGTON Fare 2/3C 026

3259 MR HARTINGTON

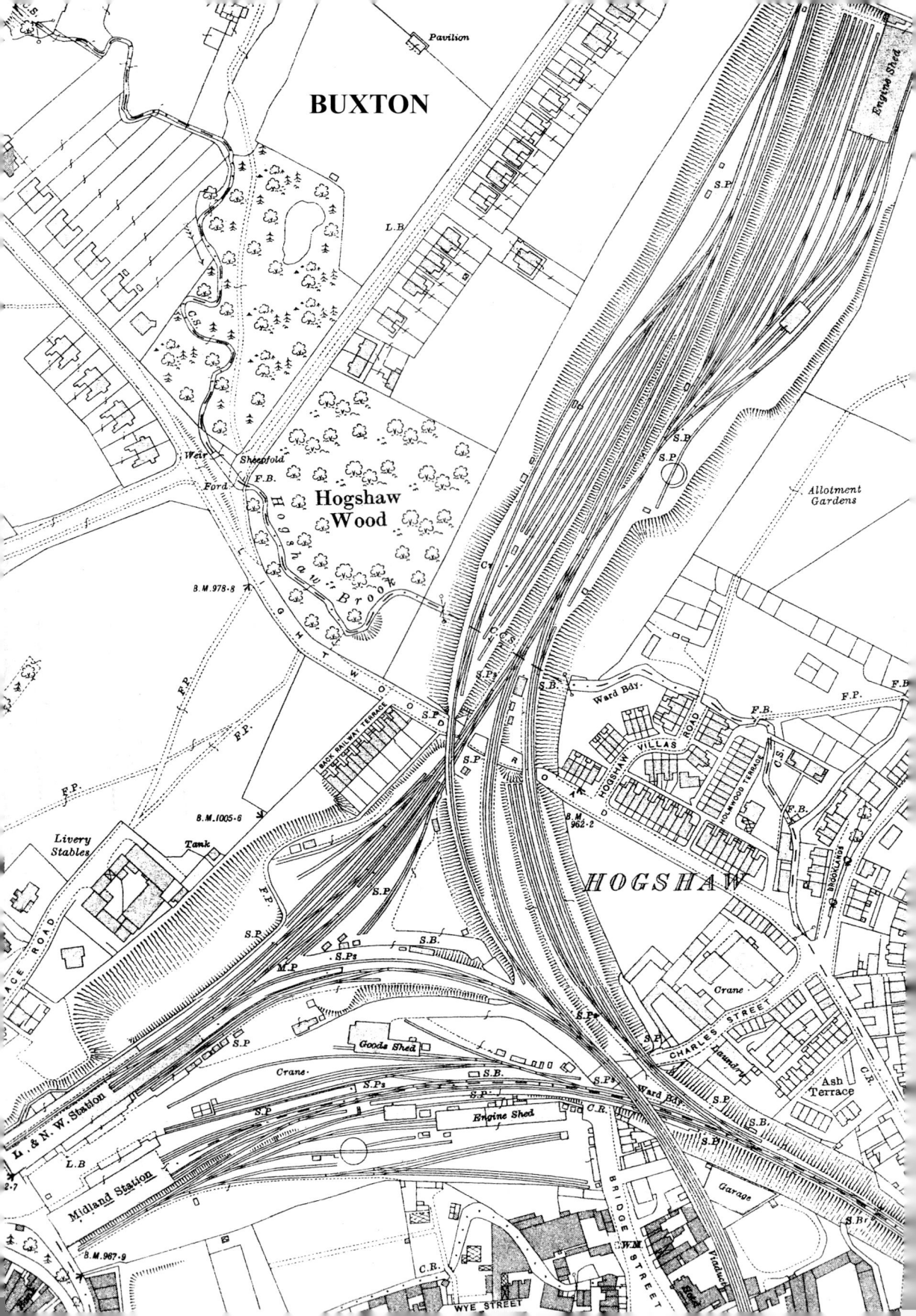

BUXTON

Pavilion

L.B.

Engine Shed

S.P.

Hogshaw
Wood

S.P.

S.P.

Allotment
Gardens

Weir
Ford
Sheepfold
F.B.

Hogshaw Brook

B.M.978·8

Ward Bdy.

F.B.
F.P.

F.B.

S.Ps

S.B.

HOGSHAW VILLAS ROAD

HOLMWOOD TERRACE

C.S.

F.B.

F.P.

BACK RAILWAY TERRACE

S.P.

S.P.

R

B.M.962·2

BROOKLANDS

F.P.

B.M.1005·6

Livery
Stables

Tank

S.P.

S.P.

HOGSHAW

F.P.

S.P.

S.B.

S.P.

Crane

M.P.

S.Ps

S.P.

S.B.

S.P.

CHARLES STREET

Laundry

C.R.

Crane

Goods Shed

S.B.

Ash
Terrace

S.Ps

S.P.

S.P.

Ward Bdy.

S.B.

L. & N.W. Station

Crane

Engine Shed

S.P.

L.B.

2·7

S.P.

C.R.

Garage

S.B.

Midland Station

BRIDGE STREET

Viaduct

W.M.

B.M.967·9

C.R.

WYE STREET

← XX. We arrive over the sharp curve which starts at the lower border of this 1922 survey, shown at 20ins to 1 mile. The LNWR terminus is the upper one, lower left. Its main line north passes its engine shed and stock sidings top right. The MR area (lower centre) was in use until 6th March 1967. The long connecting curve near HOGSHAW had been added in 1908, by the LNWR for mineral traffic. Above the MR engine shed is their isolated excursion platform, which was removed in 1932. Access to it was from Bridge Street. This engine shed was closed in August 1935. Nearby was siding space for 62 coal wagons. The turntable shown was 40ft long and was replaced by a 50ft one, east of the top engine shed, in 1935. On the left are the 1876 stables. The LNWR provided latrines at their engine shed from 1897.

104. The entrance to the space between the two terminal buildings is seen, along with most of their chimneys. The massive iron gates appear to have gone, probably to make guns for World War I with which the soldiers are likely to be involved. (P.Laming coll.)

Bradshaw advertisement, 1893.

105. This is the former LNWR side in about 1931. Nearest on the right is a 6-wheeled coach, coupled to a later 8-wheeled bogie one. The four windows on the end of the left one were for the benefit of the guard. (LOSA)

106. A 1934 shot gives a clear view of 0-6-2T no. 6912 departing for Ashbourne. We are close to 1000ft above sea level and the beautiful hills rise behind. (J.Suter coll.)

107. Both stations were provided with superb matching roofing, fine semi-circular end windows and ornate office frontages. Their openings took place on 1st June 1863. The centre trolley is carrying a livestock basket in this view from May 1953. (R.Humm coll.)

L. M. & S. R.

Issued subject to the conditions & regulations in the Cos Time Tables Books Bills & Notices

Higher Buxton to
HINDLOW

THIRD CLASS.)   3250 S)   FARE -/4½

HINDLOW

L. M. & S. R.

FOR CONDITIONS SEE NOTICES

Higher Buxton to
DOWLOW

THIRD CLASS]   3259(S)   FARE -/10½ P

DOWLOW

108. Waiting to depart to Manchester on 12th July 1955 is no. 42365, a class 4 2-6-4T. The centre track is storing empty stock, but it was known as the 'engine release road'. From left to right we have platforms 2 and 1. Nos 2 and 3 are in picture 105. (R.S.Carpenter coll.)

109. We look north on 12th July 1955 from platform 2. This was often the starting location for trains to Ashbourne and Uttoxeter. The long bridge had a single line and is left of centre on the last map. It was in use from 1894 to 1969. (R.S.Carpenter coll.)

110. A view from 11th May 1963 features the former LNWR station, long after the walls seen in picture 104 had gone in about 1927. This side of the station lost its roof in 1964 and was closed on 6th March 1967. The 'Cosy Home Show Train' exhibiting here began its journey in London in June 1962. The train toured the country to demonstrate the latest trends in solid fuel heating techniques. (J.Suter coll.)

Bradshaw, July 1910.

THE PALACE HOTEL.

TELEGRAMS:
"PALACE, BUXTON."

TELEPHONE
No. 10.

FINEST POSITION.   200 ROOMS.   ELECTRIC LIGHT.
ELEVATOR.   MOTOR GARAGE WITH PIT.

Tariff Booklet on application.   C. D. HIGGINS, Manager.

London Midland & Scottish Ry.
Issued subject to the conditions & regulations in
the Cos Time Tables Books Bills & Notices

HIGHER BUXTON TO

BUXTON

THIRD CLASS]   1040(S)   FARE -/1½
BUXTON

2429

➔ 111. It is 12th May 1967 and we are in the ex-LNWR side of the station. The goods yard closed on 1st April 1967. It had earlier had a 10-ton crane. An excursion platform was near the right border. (SLS coll.)

⬇ 112. We move on to 1969 and examine the No. 1 Box of that time. The first box at Buxton was a small building on the east side of the line adjacent to the junction to the MR. It was in use by 1880 and closed circa June 1894. A box named 'Buxton No. 1' opened around 1888, mid-way along the south side of the triangle, and was re-named 'Buxton No. 2' circa 1896. It had 72 levers and a new 70-lever frame by 1937. It closed on 29th September 1973. The box seen here opened around June 1894, named 'Buxton No. 2', had 54 levers and was renamed 'Buxton No. 1' circa 1896. The frame was later extended to 60 levers. The box was renamed 'Buxton' on 29th September 1973, and the frame was later shortened to 47 levers. The box was still in use in 2019. (R.Humm coll.)

↓ 113. On the left is the diesel depot, which was begun in 1957. Arriving on 17th September 1980 is no. 50420. It is heading a service from Manchester Piccadilly. On shed is no. 45056 and nearby are nos 40135 and M50430. The shed was out of use by 2017. (T.Heavyside)

114. A class 128 parcel unit is showing its gauge code C1. It is no. 55990 and is seen on 16th September 1980. The Midland Region used more of these than any other region. They operated from 1959 to 1991. (T.Heavyside)

ST. ANN'S HOTEL, Buxton.

Centrally situated. South aspect. Very sheltered. Electric Light. American Elevator. New Lounge.
100 Rooms. Magnificent Dining Rooms, with separate tables.

Telegraphic Address: "ANNS, BUXTON." National Telephone No. 41.

Bradshaw, July 1910.

115. No. 150150 is about to return to Blackpool on 18th August 1994. Snow plough no. ADB965308 has two lamp brackets above the artwork. The town's ring road now passes over the site of the former MR part of the station. (M.Turvey)

Other News

The Peak Rail Society created its Steam Centre using the former excursion platform site and the bridge over Bridge Street. This was in 1980. It was moved to Darley Dale during 1989 and extension to Matlock followed. The story is illustrated in the final 18 photos in our *Ambergate to Buxton* album. Other views of Buxton northwards and the Peak Forest route can be enjoyed in *Buxton to Stockport. Cromford & High Peak by Rail and Trail* is another local volume with multiple revelations.

9105

3rd-SINGLE SINGLE-3rd

Hindlow   Hindlow

Hindlow   To

Buxton   Buxton

BUXTON

9105

(M) ·17 H   FARE   ·17 H (M)

For conditions see over   For conditions see over

5170

L. M. & S. R.
FOR CONDITIONS
SEE BACK

WORKMAN

On day of issue only

THIRD CLASS

Hindlow
To   (F)
HIGHER BUXTON

5170

↑ 116. Standing in the engine shed sidings in the early 1890s is 2-4-2T no. 427. This first shed was north of the platforms, near the site of the DMU shed seen in picture 113. In their final years, these small engines ran to and from Millers Dale. (R.S.Carpenter coll.)

↗ 117. Seen in about 1906 is the extensive depot of 1892. It was expanded further in 1935, with seven more sidings, a coaling plant and ash facilities being provided. This was when the ex-MR shed closed. (J.Alsop coll.)

→ 118. The 60ft turntable was provided near the border on the right. It was worked by an engine's vacuum system, when it was being turned. This panorama is from 15th June 1952. (R.Humm coll.)

119. No. 46465, a class 2 2-6-0, is under the main water tank and projecting behind it is part of the coaling plant. The shed code was 9D in 1948-63 and 9L in 1963-68. The photo is from 20th May 1966. (Colour-Rail.com)

Bradshaw, June 1937.

120. Sad conditions prevail in June 1967, but the ash wagons and facilities seem appropriate for the last view. It includes a use for old tenders. They were used as counter balances on the Cromford & High Peak inclines; see our album of that title. Total closure took place in 1968. The allocation had been 55 in 1950. (Colour-Rail.com)

Bradshaw, March 1951.

Bradshaw, January 1955.